Sandra Lee

Money Saving Meals

This book belongs to:

. . . .

Meredith® Books Des Moines, Iowa

Copyright © 2008 Sandra Lee Semi-Homemade® All rights reserved. Printed in the U.S.A.
Library of Congress Control Number 2008922212 ISBN: 978-0-696-24056-0

Special thanks to Culinary Director Jeff Parker

24 Creamy Penne Pesto Bake

56 Barbecued Rib Hash

89 Raspberry Mustard Chicken

178 Orange- and Bourbon-Turkey Tenderloins

227 Cinnamon Roll Coffee Bombe

sem·i·home·made

adj. **1:** a stress-free solution-based formula that provides savvy shortcuts and affordable, timesaving tips for overextended do-it-yourself homemakers **2:** a quick and easy equation wherein 70% ready-made convenience products are added to 30% fresh ingredients with creative personal style, allowing homemakers to take 100% of the credit for something that looks, feels, or tastes homemade **3:** a foolproof resource for having it all—and having the time to enjoy it **4:** a method created by Sandra Lee for home, garden, crafts, beauty, food, fashion, and entertaining wherein everything looks, tastes, and feels as if it was made from scratch.

Solution-based **E**nterprise that **M**otivates, **I**nspires, and **H**elps **O**rganize and **M**anage time while **E**nriching **M**odern life by **A**dding **D**ependable shortcuts **E**very day.

dedication

For all of you unsung heroes
Always on the go
Balancing work, kids, and budgets
It's challenging, I know.

My Money Saving Meals
Help you do more with less
Two-day dinners, freeze-and-serves
Keep it low on stress.

Feed the family, throw a party
Shortcuts make mealtime fun
Semi-Homemade® is the secret
For cooking on the run.
XO—SL

Table of Contents

Chapter 1
Perfect Pantry Shortcuts
18

Chapter 3
Real-Quick Rotisserie Chicken
64

Chapter 2
Dolled-Up Deli Delights
42

Chapter 4
Fix It and Freeze It
84

Letter from Sandra

When I was very young, my Grandma Lorraine taught me that even the simplest foods are special when they're made with love. So much of what I know about food I learned from my family. Grandma taught me that a pecan crust makes chicken taste rich. Aunt Peggy and Uncle Bill showed me how to marinate a flank steak in salad dressing to turn a tough, inexpensive piece of meat into a tender meal. And my niece Stephanie pointed out that M&M's® and Skittles® are a fun way to decorate a cake. The lesson is always the same: Food is love and cooking is a way to spread it.

Of course, while the desire to prepare homemade food may always be there, the time and money sometimes aren't. Meals have become an either-or proposition: Either feed the family fast with expensive takeout, or spend hours shopping and cooking meals you can feel good about serving. Semi-Homemade® combines the best of both, with savvy shortcuts and money-saving solutions that help you make wholesome, scratch-tasting meals in minutes. It all boils down to my 70/30 philosophy: Mix 70% quality prepackaged foods with 30% fresh ingredients, add a dash of your own creativity, and cook up a meal that's 100% fast and fabulous! It's a formula that lightens the load for everyone—young and old, singles and families.

Eating well while staying on budget is easy with a little help from your friends—this book, your pantry, the deli, and the local bakery. You'll find 10 chapters of fix-it-fast recipes for every course, from appetizers and entrées to sides, desserts, and drinks. Every one is creatively fashioned from frozen, canned, or boxed foods given an infusion of fresh flavors. "Perfect Pantry Shortcuts" combines off-the-shelf staples with inexpensive vegetables and proteins for a quick, delicious dinner. "Lavish Leftovers" provides excellent, cost-conscious ideas for how to bring new life to leftover meat, poultry, and seafood. "Fix It and Freeze It" allows you to budget shop when food prices are cheaper, then cook and freeze meals so you can reheat them when time and money are short. "Cook Once Eat Thrice" helps you make the most of one night's dinner by turning it into different-tasting dishes for the following two nights.

I always make room for dessert—and time for it too—with easy-to-prepare goodies that range from barely baked to embellish and serve in the "Sweet Solutions" chapter. "Quick-Fix Holiday" pairs a dressy main course with heirloom sides, while "Party Pairings" mixes chic cocktails and appetizers into festive parties. Let my money-saving ideas and shortcuts inspire yours. I'll show you how to stock your own pantry with the building blocks of a mouthwatering meal and share practical tips that heighten the flavor of food while reducing the prep and cost. It all adds up to more choices and more meals for less time and money.

Food is a warm hug on a plate … in a bowl … in a cup. Ladle it generously and everyone in your life will drink it in. It's the quickest way to make others feel special and blessed. When we can't express what someone means to us, we can pour our heart and soul into a pork roast … corn bread casserole … tiramisu. Food says it all: "Thank you." "Welcome!" "Feel better." "You're wonderful." "I love you."

Here's to a happy, healthy life!

Sandra Lee

Dinner from the Deli

Look at fast food in a whole new way! With these grab-and-go favorites—like rotisserie chicken, mac 'n' cheese, deli salads, corn bread, and other heat-and-eat items—dinner's a cinch.

Ask the Butcher

Completely stuffed: What saves more time than already-stuffed chicken breasts, pork chops, and other meats? Just remove from the wrapping and bake!

Meal on a stick: Another fabulous timesaver is buying premade kabobs. All the cutting and threading has been done. Now just bake or grill for a supremely delicious dinner.

Twice the goodness: Twice-baked potatoes are the ultimate side dish, but when they're premade, they're twice (or thrice) as good! They're packed with plenty of flavorful add-ins; the only prep work you'll have to do is point at your favorite one in the case.

Seriously seafood: Look for shortcuts at the butcher counter. Oftentimes you can find handy helpers like peeled and deveined shrimp or cooked crab legs.

Stuffed chicken breasts and kabobs

Twice-baked potatoes

Crab and peeled, deveined shrimp

Fresh meat and seafood

9

Must-Haves in Produce

A few staples from the produce section—tomatoes, peppers, carrots, onions, and lettuce—will give you endless options for fresh additions to every meal. Use extras in lunchtime salads.

Bakery Beauties

Dinner sides: The bakery is full of irresistible favorites just waiting to serve as prep-free serve-alongs. Try a different variety every time you buy to add fantastic flair to mealtime. For instance, if you always go for French baguettes, try a sourdough loaf or challah bread at your next sit-down. Bagels, dinner rolls, flavored bread—such as garlic or Asiago cheese—are all excellent choices for lunch or supper.

Breakfast boosters: Skip cold cereal and milk—your morning meal doesn't have to be dull anymore! Add sensational flavor and interest with a variety of grab-and-go goodies from the supermarket bakery. Pair up blueberry or cranberry muffins with a brilliant selection of fresh fruit—such as sliced kiwi and strawberries. Or smear some butter on fresh croissants and serve with fried eggs and bacon.

Now for dessert: There's no better place to find quick fresh-from-the-oven sweets to relish after a light meal. Do it up right with beautiful white bakery cake—make it special with your favorite sprinkles. For parties, teas, and unexpected guests, keep some bakery cookies on hand. And for a special treat? Serve everyone a cupcake!

Cakes, cookies, cupcakes

Baguettes, bagels, bread

Muffins, rolls, croissants

Freezer Ease

Spend a day cooking and freezing meals for delicious thaw-and-eat dinners on busy nights. Just transfer soups, stews, chilies, and casseroles to air-tight containers and freeze for up to 3 months.

Minutes to Mashed

My favorite new fast-fix side dish is Ore-Ida® Steam n' Mash potatoes—just pop in the microwave, then mash to perfection. Steam n' Mash russet potatoes are the perfect side dish for any meat, fish, or poultry dish—plus they can make the holidays supereasy. For extra flavor, try the following stir-ins:

- Roasted garlic
- Pesto
- Bacon and blue cheese
- Horseradish
- Sour cream and fresh chives
- Cheddar cheese and horseradish
- Dijon mustard and fresh herbs
- Buttermilk
- Stone-ground mustard and herbes de Provence

Don't forget Steam n' Mash sweet potatoes always make meals special. For added flavor, embellish with one or more of the following ingredients:

- Cilantro
- Maple syrup
- BBQ sauce and french-fried onions (as a topper)
- Green onion
- Red pepper flakes
- Cinnamon or nutmeg
- Chopped chipotle peppers

Also try Steam n' Mash potatoes to make potato pancakes or to top shepherd's pies.

Steam n' Mash sweet potatoes and stir-ins

Separate food layers with waxed paper

Freeze leftover soup

Stock Your Shelves

Think of the supermarket as your own personal sous-chef!
When you pack your cupboards with a variety of convenience
foods and pantry staples, dinner will be a snap every night.

Go-To Pantry

Keep it cold: Items like olives, roasted red peppers, artichoke hearts, and marinated vegetables can be stored in the refrigerator. Add them to salads and omelets for extra flavor. Jarred fruit makes quick snacks.

From the pantry: Pasta, rice, couscous, marinara, broth, and salad dressing are all must-haves for every pantry.

Pesto power: Basil pesto is the one item every pantry should have. It's a simple and delicious stir-in for pasta, salads, and sauces. It's also divine as a spread for crusty bread. Other similar products to keep on hand are olive tapenade, jarred bruschetta, and sun-dried tomato pesto.

Spice it up: McCormick® has some great new spice blends for quick flavor. For example, coat meat in Crusting Blends for delicious flavor and crunch.

Basil and tomato pesto, olive tapenade, and jarred bruschetta

Herbs and spices

Refrigerated pantry items   Delicious deli items

15

Sandra's Basic Pantry List

Dry Pantry
- ❏ Rice (instant, converted)
- ❏ Canned diced tomatoes (assorted flavors and types)
- ❏ Canned artichoke hearts
- ❏ Canned reduced-sodium chicken broth
- ❏ Canned reduced-sodium beef broth
- ❏ Canned reduced-sodium vegetable broth
- ❏ Canned mexicorn
- ❏ Canned sliced black olives
- ❏ Canned ham
- ❏ Canned chicken
- ❏ Canned shrimp
- ❏ Canned solid white tuna
- ❏ Canned skinless, boneless salmon
- ❏ Condensed tomato soup
- ❏ Condensed cheese soup
- ❏ Assorted seasoned bread crumbs
- ❏ Dried pasta
- ❏ Jarred pesto
- ❏ Jarred Alfredo sauce
- ❏ Jarred roasted red peppers
- ❏ Extra virgin olive oil
- ❏ Canola oil
- ❏ Nonstick cooking spray
- ❏ Balsamic vinegar
- ❏ Stir-fry sauce
- ❏ Soy sauce
- ❏ Ramen noodle packages
- ❏ Boxed macaroni and cheese
- ❏ Soft white bread

Frozen
- ❏ Frozen meatballs
- ❏ Frozen seasoning blend
- ❏ Frozen vegetables (carrots, green peppers, green beans, mixed vegetables, stir-fry mix)
- ❏ Frozen onions (chopped and pearl)
- ❏ Frozen mashed potatoes (*Ore-Ida® Steam n' Mash*)
- ❏ Frozen french fries
- ❏ Frozen bread dough
- ❏ Frozen cooked shrimp

Refrigerated
- ❏ Lemon juice
- ❏ Eggs
- ❏ Grated Parmesan cheese
- ❏ Mayonnaise
- ❏ Dijon mustard
- ❏ Scallions (green onions)
- ❏ Celery
- ❏ Sour cream
- ❏ Butter

Seasonings and Spices
- ❏ Salt
- ❏ Ground black pepper
- ❏ Garlic salt
- ❏ Garlic powder
- ❏ Herbes de Provence
- ❏ Red pepper flakes
- ❏ Bottled crushed garlic
- ❏ Dried oregano
- ❏ Dried basil

Perfect Pantry Shortcuts

1. Stock your pantry well. Add a protein (meat or soy substitute) and/or fresh vegetables to pantry staples and you can create a delicious, wholesome meal in minutes.

2. Choose double-duty foods. Olives, pickles, pearl onions, pineapples, cherries and peaches can serve as flavor enhancers as well as food and cocktail garnishes.

3. Think small. Buy good-quality herbs and spices in the smallest containers possible. Date them and alphabetize on inside-the-door racks. Discard after six months.

4. Get milk. Evaporated milk has 60 percent less water. Swap it for regular milk to make a dish richer and creamier. Powdered milk is thrifty for cooking—it works exactly the same in recipes.

5. Group like with like. Store flour, sugar, and shortening with sweet spices in one area; savory spices, sauces, and marinades in another. Stack food on risers and in clear, airtight containers so you won't waste time searching for ingredients.

The Recipes

Greek Chicken and Rice

Prep 25 minutes   **Bake** 40 minutes
Makes 4 servings

SHOPPING LIST

- Boneless, skinless chicken breasts
- Greek seasoning
- Frozen chopped spinach
- Kalamata olives
- Crumbled feta with garlic herbs

4	(6 ounces each) boneless, skinless chicken breasts, trimmed of fat
2	teaspoons Greek seasoning, *McCormick®*
1	teaspoon garlic salt, *Lawry's®*
	Nonstick cooking spray, *Pam®*
1	can (14-ounce) petite diced tomatoes with garlic and olive oil, drained, *Del Monte®*
1	can (13.75-ounce) artichoke quarters, drained and rinsed, *Maria®*
1	box (10-ounce) frozen chopped spinach, cooked and well drained, *C&W®*
1	cup converted rice, *Uncle Ben's®*
1	cup frozen onions, *Ore-Ida®*
2	tablespoons lemon juice, *Minute Maid®*
2	cups reduced-sodium chicken broth, *Swanson®*
⅓	cup pitted kalamata olives, *Peloponnese®*
1	package (4-ounce) crumbled feta with garlic and herbs, *Athenos®*

1. Preheat oven to 375 degrees F. Season chicken breasts with Greek seasoning and garlic salt. Spray a large skillet with cooking spray; add chicken. Cook chicken for 4 to 6 minutes or until browned, turning once. Set aside.

2. In a large bowl, combine tomatoes, artichokes, spinach, uncooked rice, onions, and lemon juice. Transfer to a 9×13-inch baking dish. Push chicken breasts down into rice mixture.

3. Pour broth over top of chicken; top with olives and sprinkle with feta. Cover with aluminum foil and bake in preheated oven for 40 to 45 minutes or until liquid has been absorbed.

Enchilada Lasagna

Prep 30 minutes   **Bake** 40 minutes
Stand 5 minutes

1	can (16-ounce) refried black beans, *Rosarita*®
1	can (4-ounce) diced green chiles, *Ortega*®
1	container (15-ounce) ricotta, *Precious*®
1	egg, lightly beaten
2	teaspoons Mexican seasoning, *McCormick*®
½	teaspoon salt
2	cans (10 ounces each) red enchilada sauce, *Las Palmas*®
18	corn tortillas
1	can (11-ounce) mexicorn, drained, *Green Giant*®
2	packages (6 ounces each) grilled chicken strips, cut into bite-size pieces, *Tyson*®
3	cups shredded Mexican blend cheese, *Sargento*®
	Sour cream (optional)
	Sliced scallion (green onion) (optional)

SHOPPING LIST
- ■ Canned refried black beans
- ■ Canned diced green chiles
- ■ Ricotta cheese
- ■ Mexican seasoning
- ■ Red enchilada sauce
- ■ Corn tortillas
- ■ Grilled chicken strips
- ■ Mexican cheese blend

1. Preheat oven to 400 degrees F. In a medium microwave-safe bowl, combine refried black beans and diced green chiles. Cover and microwave on high setting (100 percent power) for 1 minute. Set aside. In a small bowl, stir together ricotta, egg, Mexican seasoning, and salt.

2. Spread ½ cup of the enchilada sauce evenly in a 9×13-inch baking pan. Overlap 6 corn tortillas to create a layer. Spread half of the black bean mixture evenly over tortillas. Top with half of the ricotta mixture, spreading evenly. Sprinkle with half of the mexicorn, one package of the chicken, and 1 cup of the shredded cheese. Spread ½ cup of the enchilada sauce over top. Add another layer of tortillas; top with ¼ cup of the enchilada sauce. Repeat with remaining black bean mixture, remaining ricotta mixture, remaining mexicorn, remaining chicken, another 1 cup of the shredded cheese, another ½ cup of the enchilada sauce, and the remaining tortillas. Spread remaining enchilada sauce over tortillas and sprinkle with remaining shredded cheese.

3. Cover with aluminum foil and bake in preheated oven for 40 to 45 minutes or until bubbly. Let rest for 5 minutes before serving. Serve with sour cream and sliced scallion (optional).

Creamy Penne Pesto Bake

Prep 25 minutes **Bake** 30 minutes
Makes 4 servings

SHOPPING LIST
- Italian cheese blend
- Grilled chicken strips

	Nonstick cooking spray, *Pam*®
8	ounces penne pasta, *Barilla*®
1½	cups Alfredo sauce, *Classico*®
1	jar (5-ounce) pesto sauce, *Classico*®
1	can (13.75-ounce) artichoke hearts, drained and rinsed, *Maria*®
2	cups shredded Italian cheese blend, *Sargento*®
2	packets (6 ounces each) grilled chicken strips, *Tyson*®
½	cup roasted red peppers, chopped, *Delallo*®
¼	cup Italian bread crumbs, *Progresso*®
¼	cup grated Parmesan cheese, *DiGiorno*®
1½	teaspoons extra virgin olive oil, *Bertolli*®

1. Preheat oven to 375 degrees F. Lightly spray a 2½-quart casserole dish with cooking spray; set aside.

2. In a large saucepan of boiling salted water, cook pasta for 1 minute less than directed on package. Drain and set aside.

3. For creamy pesto, in a medium bowl, stir together Alfredo sauce and pesto sauce; set aside.

4. In a large bowl, toss to combine artichoke hearts, Italian cheese blend, chicken, and roasted red peppers. Add cooked pasta and creamy pesto; using a rubber spatula, fold together until well mixed. Transfer to prepared casserole dish.

5. In a small bowl, combine bread crumbs, Parmesan cheese, and oil; sprinkle over pasta. Bake in preheated oven for 30 to 45 minutes or until golden brown and bubbling.

Open-Face Chicken Basil Sandwiches

Start to Finish 20 minutes
Makes 4 servings

2	cans (5 ounces each) chicken breast, drained, *Valley Fresh*®
1	stalk celery, chopped
1	scallion (green onion), finely chopped
1	tablespoon finely chopped fresh basil leaves
¼	cup sour cream
2	tablespoons mayonnaise, *Hellmann's*® or *Best Foods*®
1	teaspoon Dijon mustard, *Grey Poupon*®
1	teaspoon lemon juice, *Minute Maid*®
1	teaspoon salt-free lemon pepper, *The Spice Hunter*®
4	slices soft white bread
	Additional fresh basil leaves and sprigs (optional)

SHOPPING LIST
■ Fresh basil
■ Salt-free lemon pepper seasoning

1. In a medium bowl, break chicken into bite-size pieces. Gently stir in celery, scallion, and basil. In a small bowl, stir together sour cream, mayonnaise, Dijon mustard, lemon juice, and lemon pepper. Pour sour cream mixture over chicken mixture; stir just until combined.

2. Trim crusts from bread slices; toast slices in a toaster. Place additional basil leaves on toast (optional). Spoon chicken mixture onto bread, spreading evenly. Garnish each sandwich with a sprig of basil (optional).

Cashew Chicken Stir-Fried Noodles

Start to Finish 25 minutes
Makes 4 servings

SHOPPING LIST
- Chopped ginger
- Boneless, skinless chicken breasts
- Sliced water chestnuts
- Cashews

¾ cup stir-fry sauce, *House of Tsang®*
2 packages (3 ounces each) chicken-flavor ramen noodles, *Top Ramen®*
1 tablespoon chopped ginger, *Gourmet Garden®*
2 tablespoons canola oil
1¼ pounds boneless, skinless chicken breasts, cut into bite-size pieces
1 can (8-ounce) sliced water chestnuts, *Dynasty®*
1 cup chopped celery
1 cup frozen seasoning blend vegetables, *Pictsweet®*
1 cup cashews, *Planters®*

1. For sauce, in a small bowl, stir together stir-fry sauce, seasoning packets from ramen noodles, and ginger. Set aside. In a medium saucepan, cook ramen noodles following package directions. Drain.

2. In a large skillet, heat oil over high heat. Add chicken; stir-fry for 4 to 5 minutes. Add water chestnuts, celery, and vegetable blend; stir-fry for 2 minutes more. Add cooked, drained ramen noodles; stir-fry for 3 minutes or until noodles, chicken, and vegetables are combined and heated through. Pour in sauce; add cashews. Stir-fry for 2 to 3 minutes or until sauce is mostly absorbed.

Ham Fried Rice

Start to Finish 25 minutes
Makes 6 servings

SHOPPING LIST
- Szechuan seasoning
- Frozen mixed vegetables
- Toasted sesame oil

2 cups instant rice, *Uncle Ben's®*
2 cups reduced-sodium chicken broth, *Swanson®*
1 teaspoon Szechuan seasoning, *Spice Islands®*
2 tablespoons canola oil
2½ cups frozen mixed vegetables, *C&W®*
2 cans (5 ounces each) chunk-style ham, *Hormel®*
1 can (4-ounce) tiny shrimp, *Chicken of the Sea®*
2 teaspoons toasted sesame oil
2 eggs, lightly beaten
1 tablespoon soy sauce, *Kikkoman®*
3 scallions (green onions), thinly sliced (optional)

1. In a saucepan, combine uncooked rice, broth, and Szechuan seasoning. Bring to a boil. Cover; remove from heat. Let stand for 5 to 7 minutes or until rice is tender and liquid is almost absorbed. Fluff with fork.

2. In a large skillet or wok, heat oil over medium-high heat. Add cooked rice, frozen vegetables, ham, and shrimp; stir-fry for 3 to 5 minutes or until vegetables and ham are heated through. Make a well in the center of the rice mixture; pour sesame oil into the well. Heat through. Add eggs; scramble eggs with rice mixture. Add soy sauce; stir rice to combine. Garnish with sliced scallions (optional).

Coconut Curry Pork

Prep 15 minutes   **Cook** 11 minutes
Makes 6 servings

Caribbean or Thai, this vibrant summery dish tastes warm and tropical year-round. Sweet, creamy coconut milk cuts curry's spiciness, while canned fruits and veggies help create an easy open-and-serve meal. To make a vegetarian version, substitute tofu for pork.

2	packages (17 ounces each) prepared pork roast au jus, *Hormel*®
2	tablespoons canola oil
2	tablespoons red curry paste, *Thai Kitchen*®
1	can (15-ounce) sweet potatoes, *Princella*®
1½	cups reduced-sodium chicken broth, *Swanson*®
1	can (8-ounce) pineapple chunks, *Dole*®
1	cup frozen chopped green bell pepper, *Pictsweet*®
1	cup frozen chopped onion, *Ore-Ida*®
1½	cups unsweetened coconut milk, *Thai Kitchen*®
¼	cup finely chopped fresh cilantro
	Hot cooked rice
	Chopped cilantro and/or chopped macadamia nuts

SHOPPING LIST
- Prepared pork roast au jus
- Red curry paste
- Canned sweet potatoes
- Canned pineapple chunks
- Coconut milk
- Fresh cilantro
- Macadamia nuts (optional)

1. Remove pork roast from package and chop into bite-size pieces; set aside. Discard tray juices.

2. In a large skillet, heat oil over medium-high heat. Add curry paste; fry for 1 minute. Stir in sweet potatoes, broth, pineapple chunks, green pepper, and onion. Bring to a boil; reduce heat. Simmer, uncovered, for 10 minutes. Stir in coconut milk and cilantro; cook about 1 minute longer or until heated through.

3. Serve over hot cooked rice. Garnish with chopped cilantro and/or chopped macadamia nuts (optional).

Polynesian Pork
with Pineapple Rice

Prep 20 minutes   **Bake** 40 minutes
Makes 4 servings

SHOPPING LIST
- Pork chops
- Teriyaki marinade mix
- Canned crushed pineapple
- Pineapple juice

1½ pounds thick-cut boneless pork chops, trimmed
4 teaspoons teriyaki marinade mix, *Sun Bird*®
2 tablespoons canola oil
1 bag (14-ounce) frozen stir-fry vegetables, *C&W*®
2 cups instant rice, *Uncle Ben's*®
1 can (8-ounce) crushed pineapple, *Dole*®
1¼ cups reduced-sodium chicken broth, *Swanson*®
¾ cup pineapple juice, *Dole*®
  Coarsely chopped cashews (optional)

1. Preheat oven to 375 degrees F. Cut pork chops into bite-size pieces; toss with 2 teaspoons of the teriyaki mix. In a large skillet, heat oil over medium-high heat. Add pork to hot oil; cook for 3 to 4 minutes or until browned on all sides. Add stir-fry vegetables; toss to combine. Set aside.

2. In a 2½-quart casserole dish, combine uncooked rice, undrained pineapple, broth, pineapple juice, and the remaining 2 teaspoons teriyaki mix; stir until well mixed.

3. Spoon pork, vegetables, and any cooking juices over the rice mixture. Cover and bake in preheated oven for 40 to 45 minutes or until rice is tender and liquid is almost absorbed. Garnish with chopped cashews (optional).

Cheesy Jambalaya

Prep 20 minutes   **Bake** 30 minutes
Makes 4 servings

Nonstick cooking spray, *Pam®*
1   box (12-ounce) shells and cheese, *Velveeta®*
2   teaspoons Cajun seasoning, *McCormick®*
1   can (14-ounce) diced tomatoes with green bell peppers and onions, drained, *Del Monte®*
1   can (10.75-ounce) condensed cheddar cheese soup, *Campbell's®*
2   cups Cajun-style andouille sausage (about 10 ounces), *Aidells®*
1   cup frozen seasoning blend vegetables, *Pictsweet®*
1   can (5-ounce) chicken breast, drained and rinsed, *Valley Fresh®*
1   can (4-ounce) shrimp, drained and rinsed, *Chicken of the Sea®*
½   cup garlic and herb bread crumbs, *Progresso®*
1½ teaspoons extra virgin olive oil, *Bertolli®*
    Snipped fresh Italian parsley (optional)

SHOPPING LIST
- Cajun seasoning
- Cajun-style andouille sausage

1. Preheat oven to 375 degrees F. Lightly spray a 2½-quart casserole dish with cooking spray; set aside.

2. In a large saucepan of boiling water, cook pasta shells for 8 minutes. Drain and return pasta to hot saucepan. Stir in cheese pouch and Cajun seasoning; set aside.

3. While pasta is cooking, in a large bowl, combine tomatoes, cheese soup, sausage, vegetable blend, chicken breast, and shrimp. Set aside. In a small bowl, stir together bread crumbs and oil; set aside.

4. Using a rubber spatula, fold pasta-cheese mixture into the sausage mixture. Transfer to prepared casserole dish. Sprinkle with bread crumbs mixture. Bake in preheated oven for 30 to 40 minutes or until golden brown and bubbling. Garnish with snipped parsley (optional).

Red Wine Beef over Herbed Polenta

Prep 25 minutes   **Cook** 10 minutes
Makes 6 servings

Polenta has a stronger taste than rice, so it holds its own with pungent blue cheese. Using premade polenta takes only five minutes—a fraction of the time it would take from scratch. The rich evaporated milk keeps it from drying out and balances the beef's heartiness.

SHOPPING LIST
- Refrigerated cooked polenta
- Evaporated milk
- Bacon crumbles
- Jarred whole mushrooms
- Red wine
- Crumbled blue cheese

FOR HERBED POLENTA:

1	package (24-ounce) refrigerated cooked polenta, *San Gennaro*®
½	cup evaporated milk, *Carnation*®
½	cup reduced-sodium chicken broth, *Swanson*®
¼	cup crumbled real bacon, *Hormel*®
1	teaspoon herbes de Provence, *McCormick*®

FOR RED WINE BEEF:

36	frozen meatballs, *Rosina*®
1	bag (14-ounce) frozen pearl onions, *C&W*®
2	cups frozen sliced carrots, *C&W*®
1	can (14.5-ounce) diced tomatoes with basil, garlic, and onions, *Hunt's*®
1	can (10-ounce) condensed tomato soup, *Campbell's*®
2	jars (4.5 ounces each) whole mushrooms, drained and rinsed, *Green Giant*®
1	cup red wine (Cabernet Sauvignon)
2	teaspoons herbes de Provence, *McCormick*®
	Salt and black pepper
	Crumbled blue cheese (optional), *Sargento*®

1. For Herbed Polenta, break up polenta into a medium saucepan. Add evaporated milk, broth, crumbled bacon, and herbes. Bring to a simmer over medium heat. Using a wooden spoon, mash polenta until creamy. Cover and set aside.

2. For Red Wine Beef, in a large straight-side skillet or Dutch oven, combine meatballs, onions, carrots, tomatoes, tomato soup, mushrooms, red wine, and herbes. Cover and bring to a boil over medium heat; reduce heat. Simmer for 10 minutes. Season to taste with salt and pepper. Serve hot over Herbed Polenta. Sprinkle with blue cheese (optional).

Nouvelle Niçoise Bake

Prep 15 minutes   **Bake** 35 minutes
Makes 6 servings

Nonstick cooking spray, *Pam*®
4   cups refrigerated precooked potatoes with herbs and garlic, *Reeser's*®
2   cans (12 ounces each) solid white tuna, drained, *Starkist*®
1½ cups frozen cut green beans, *Birds Eye*®
½   cup sliced black olives, *Early California*®
2   cans (10 ounces each) prepared white sauce, *Aunt Penny's*®
1   can (14-ounce) diced tomatoes, *Hunt's*®
2   teaspoons herbes de Provence, *McCormick*®
1½ cups panko bread crumbs, *Ian's*®
2   tablespoons extra virgin olive oil, *Bertolli*®

SHOPPING LIST
- Refrigerated precooked potatoes with herbs and garlic
- Prepared white sauce
- Panko bread crumbs

1. Preheat oven to 400 degrees F. Lightly spray a 3- to 4-quart shallow baking dish with cooking spray. Spread potatoes in baking dish. Set aside.

2. In a large bowl, combine drained tuna, green beans, and olives. In a medium bowl, stir together white sauce, tomatoes, and herbes. Fold into tuna mixture. Pour over potatoes; spread evenly.

3. In a small bowl, stir together bread crumbs and oil; sprinkle evenly over casserole. Bake in preheated oven for 35 to 45 minutes or until golden brown and bubbling.

Shepherd's Pie

Prep 20 minutes   **Bake** 30 minutes
Makes 8 servings

Nonstick cooking spray, *Pam*®
4   slices bacon
1½ pounds beef stew meat
1   onion, chopped
2   cups mixed frozen vegetables, *Birds Eye*®
1   jar (12-ounce) beef gravy, *Heinz*®
1   cup reduced-sodium beef broth, *Swanson*®
1   packet (1.25-ounce) peppercorn gravy mix, *McCormick*®
1   package (24-ounce) frozen mashed potatoes, *Ore-Ida*® *Steam n' Mash*
¼   cup sour cream
1   tablespoon prepared horseradish
1   teaspoon Worcestershire sauce, *Lea & Perrins*®

SHOPPING LIST
- Bacon
- Beef stew meat
- Peppercorn gravy mix
- Prepared horseradish

1. Preheat oven to 350 degrees F. Lightly spray a shallow 9×13-inch baking dish or casserole with cooking spray; set aside. In a large skillet, fry bacon over medium heat until browned but not crispy. Remove with a slotted spoon to plate lined with paper towels. Drain all but 2 tablespoons of the fat from the pan. Add stew meat and brown on all sides. Add onions; cook for 2 minutes more. Stir in vegetables, cooked bacon, gravy, broth, and peppercorn gravy mix. Bring to a boil and reduce to simmer for 1 minute.

2. Transfer to prepared baking dish and set aside. Prepare mashed potatoes according to package directions. Stir in sour cream, horseradish, and Worcestershire sauce. Distribute scoops of potato mixture evenly over stew. Bake in preheated oven for 30 to 40 minutes or until hot and bubbly. Serve hot.

Salmon Cakes with Salsa

Prep 20 minutes **Bake** 20 minutes
Makes 4 servings

SHOPPING LIST
- ■ Diced pimiento
- ■ Salt-free seafood seasoning
- ■ Jarred olive bruschetta
- ■ Fresh flat-leaf parsley

FOR SALMON CAKES:

Nonstick cooking spray, *Pam®*

3 cans (6 ounces each) skinless, boneless canned salmon, drained and rinsed, *Demings®*

1 tablespoon lemon juice, *Minute Maid®*

¾ cup mayonnaise, *Hellmann's®* or *Best Foods®*

¾ cup seasoned bread crumbs, *Progresso®*

½ cup frozen seasoning blend vegetables, thawed, *Pictsweet®*

1 jar (2-ounce) diced pimiento, drained, *Dromedary®*

1 tablespoon finely chopped fresh flat-leaf parsley

2 teaspoons salt-free seafood seasoning, *The Spice Hunter®*

FOR SALSA:

1 can (15-ounce) petite diced tomatoes, *S&W®*

½ cup olive bruschetta, *Delallo®*

2 tablespoons finely chopped fresh flat-leaf parsley

1 tablespoon balsamic vinegar

1 teaspoon salt

1 teaspoon crushed garlic, *Gourmet Garden®*

½ teaspoon red pepper flakes, *McCormick®*

1. Preheat oven to 400 degrees F. Generously spray a baking sheet with cooking spray; set aside.

2. In a large bowl, toss together salmon and lemon juice, breaking apart salmon. Add mayonnaise, ¼ cup of the bread crumbs, the vegetable blend, pimiento, parsley, and seafood seasoning; fold together with a rubber spatula just until blended.

3. Spread the remaining ½ cup bread crumbs on a plate. Form 8 cakes from salmon mixture; dredge in bread crumbs. Place on prepared baking sheet. Spray cakes with cooking spray. Bake for 20 minutes, turning halfway through baking time.

4. For the salsa, in a medium bowl, combine diced tomatoes, olive bruschetta, parsley, balsamic vinegar, salt, garlic, and red pepper flakes. Serve hot salmon cakes with salsa.

Dolled-Up Deli Delights

1. Take dishes to the next level. Drizzle flavored oils and vinegars over cheeses, roasted vegetables, and salads as a finishing touch. Use less pricey selections for marinades and dressings.

2. Give it a garnish. A sprig of dill, a sprinkle of paprika, or a few pickles or capers add flavor and color to purchased salads. Crush dried herbs between your fingers to release the aromatic oils before topping off your dish.

3. Be clever with condiments. Spice up plain mayonnaise with sun-dried tomatoes, chipotle peppers, dried or fresh herbs, or mustards, such as stone-ground or Dijon.

4. Go gourmet. Two tablespoons of prepared pesto gives a cup of deli chicken salad a whole new flavor.

5. Feed a crowd. Line up white, whole wheat, and sourdough bread; a platter of cold cuts and cheeses; salad bar greens; and creative condiments and make it a sandwich bar.

The Recipes

Hot Buffalo Chicken Dip

Prep 10 minutes **Bake** 45 minutes
Makes 4 cups dip

Olive oil cooking spray, *Pam®*
8   ounces cream cheese, softened, *Philadelphia®*
½   cup hot wing sauce, *Frank's® Red Hot®*
½   cup sour cream
1   tablespoon ranch dressing mix, *Hidden Valley®*
3   cups chicken salad from the deli
1¼   cups shredded pepper jack cheese, *Tillamook®*
     Assorted dippers, such as celery sticks, bread sticks,
         and/or tortilla chips

1. Preheat oven to 325 degrees F. Lightly spray a 1-quart casserole dish with cooking spray; set aside.

2. In a medium bowl, combine cream cheese, wing sauce, sour cream, and ranch dressing mix, stirring until smooth. Fold in chicken salad and cheese.

3. Transfer to prepared casserole dish. Bake in preheated oven for 45 to 55 minutes or until heated through and bubbling. Serve warm with assorted dippers.

Curried Crab Canapés

Start to Finish 15 minutes
Makes 1½ cups

Everybody needs at least one no-cook appetizer in their repertoire, and this one is goof-proof. A carton of egg salad, a can of crabmeat, and a sprinkle of spices, and you have a stylish five-minute hors d'oeuvre. Serve on cucumber slices for parties.

1   can (6-ounce) lump crabmeat, drained and rinsed, *Crown Prince®*
1   cup egg salad from deli (about ½ pound)
1   jar (2-ounce) chopped pimiento, drained and rinsed, *Dromedary®*
½   teaspoon curry powder, *McCormick®*
½   teaspoon lemon juice, *Minute Maid®*
     Melba toast or water crackers
2   teaspoons chopped fresh chives

1. In a medium bowl, fold together crabmeat, egg salad, pimiento, curry powder, and lemon juice.

2. Spread each melba toast piece with 1 to 2 teaspoons of the egg-crab mixture. Sprinkle with chopped chives.

Tuna Cakes
with Salsa

Prep 20 minutes   Chill 1 hour
Cook 6 minutes   Makes 4 servings

FOR TUNA CAKES:

1½	cups tuna salad from deli
1	tablespoon fresh cilantro, freshly chopped
1	tablespoon lemon juice, *Minute Maid*®
2	teaspoons chopped chipotle chiles in adobo, *Embassa*®
1	teaspoon salt-free fajita seasoning, *The Spice Hunter*®
1	box (8.5-ounce) corn muffin mix, *Jiffy*®
3	tablespoons canola oil

FOR SALSA:

1	cup salsa verde, *Pace*®
¼	cup fresh cilantro, finely chopped
2	scallions (green onions), finely chopped
1	tablespoon lemon juice, *Minute Maid*®

1. For Tuna Cakes, in a medium bowl, stir together tuna salad, cilantro, lemon juice, chipotles, and fajita seasoning. Add ⅔ cup of the dry muffin mix, folding just until combined.

2. Sprinkle half of the remaining dry corn muffin mix into a 9×13-inch baking pan or onto a platter. Wet hands and form 8 tuna cakes; set tuna cakes on top of corn muffin mix. Sprinkle remaining dry corn muffin mix over cakes and refrigerate for 1 hour.

3. For the salsa, in a small bowl, stir together salsa verde, cilantro, scallions, and lemon juice. Set aside until ready to serve.

4. In a large skillet, heat oil over medium heat. Carefully add tuna cakes to hot oil; fry for 6 to 8 minutes or until golden brown and heated through, carefully turning once. Serve hot tuna cakes with salsa.

French-Style Potato Salad

Start to Finish 20 minutes
Makes 10 servings

1	quart potato or macaroni salad from deli
¼	pound thickly sliced cooked turkey breast from deli, chopped
1	cup frozen cut green beans, thawed, *C&W®*
2	hard-cooked eggs, chopped
¼	cup pitted kalamata olives, chopped, *Peloponnese®*
¼	cup red wine vinaigrette, *Wish-Bone®*
2	tablespoons Dijon mustard, *Grey Poupon®*
2	teaspoons herbes de Provence, *McCormick®*

1. In a large bowl, use a rubber spatula to gently fold together potato salad, turkey, green beans, hard-cooked eggs, olives, vinaigrette, mustard, and herbes.

Greek-Style Potato Salad

Start to Finish 20 minutes
Makes 10 servings

1	quart potato or macaroni salad from deli
1	package (4-ounce) feta cheese, *Athenos®*
⅓	cup chopped red onion
¼	cup sun-dried tomatoes, chopped, *California®*
¼	cup pitted kalamata olives, *Peloponnese®*
2	tablespoons lemon juice, *Minute Maid®*
1	tablespoon Greek seasoning, *McCormick®*
1	teaspoon crushed garlic, *Gourmet Garden®*
	Snipped fresh oregano (optional)

1. In a large bowl, use a rubber spatula to gently fold together potato salad, feta cheese, red onions, sun-dried tomatoes, olives, lemon juice, Greek seasoning, and garlic. Garnish with snipped fresh oregano (optional).

Southwest Macaroni Salad

Start to Finish 15 minutes
Makes 10 servings

1	quart macaroni or potato salad from deli
1	can (11-ounce) mexicorn, drained, *Green Giant®*
1	can (10-ounce) Mexican style tomatoes, drained, *Ro-Tel®*
⅓	cup real bacon pieces, *Hormel®*
¼	cup nacho rings (sliced jalapeño chiles), chopped, *Ortega®*
1	tablespoon Tex-Mex chili seasoning, *McCormick®*

1. In a large bowl, use a rubber spatula to gently fold together macaroni salad, mexicorn, tomatoes, bacon, nacho rings, and chili seasoning.

Creole Macaroni Salad

Start to Finish 15 minutes
Makes 10 servings

1	quart macaroni or potato salad from deli
½	pound cooked baby shrimp (about 1 cup)
1	cup chopped precooked Louisiana-style sausage, *Farmer John®*
½	cup frozen chopped onions, thawed, *Ore-Ida®*
½	cup frozen chopped green bell pepper, thawed, *Pictsweet®*
½	cup chopped celery
2	tablespoons Creole mustard, *Zatarain's®*
1	tablespoon hot pepper sauce, *Tabasco®*
2	teaspoons Cajun seasoning, *McCormick®*

1. In a large bowl, use a rubber spatula to gently fold together macaroni salad, shrimp, sausage, onions, green peppers, celery, mustard, hot pepper sauce, and Cajun seasoning.

Mac 'n' Cheeseburger Pie

Prep 20 minutes   **Bake** 35 minutes
Makes 8 servings

1	1-pound meat loaf from deli, coarsely chopped
1	can (10.75-ounce) condensed golden mushroom soup, *Campbell's*®
3	tablespoons yellow mustard, *French's*®
2	tablespoons ketchup, *Heinz*®
1	frozen 9-inch pie shell*
⅓	cup real crumbled bacon, *Hormel*®
1	container (1-pound) macaroni and cheese from deli
1	cup canned french-fried onions, *French's*®

1. Preheat oven to 375 degrees F. In a medium bowl, stir together chopped meat loaf, soup, mustard, and ketchup; press into bottom of unbaked pie shell. Set aside.

2. Stir bacon crumbles into macaroni and cheese. Spoon evenly over meat mixture; top with french-fried onions. Bake in preheated oven for 35 to 40 minutes. Slice and serve hot.

*NOTE: You can also use a deep-dish pie shell for this recipe.

Southwestern Creamed Beef

Prep 20 minutes   **Bake** 45 minutes
Makes 6 servings

Olive oil cooking spray, *Pam®*
1   pound red potatoes, cut into bite-size pieces
½   pound thickly sliced roast beef from deli, chopped
1   can (11-ounce) mexicorn, drained, *Green Giant®*
¼   cup real bacon pieces, *Hormel®*
1   can (10.75-ounce) condensed cream of potato soup, *Campbell's®*
1   cup sour cream
1   can (4-ounce) diced green chiles, *Ortega®*
1   packet (1.25-ounce) fajita seasoning mix or taco seasoning
         mix, *Ortega®*
1   cup shredded pepper Jack cheese, *Tillamook®*

1. Preheat oven to 350 degrees F. Lightly spray a 2½-quart casserole dish with cooking spray; set aside.

2. In a large bowl, toss together potato pieces, roast beef, corn, and bacon pieces.

3. In a medium bowl, stir together soup, sour cream, chiles, and seasoning mix; fold into potato mixture. Transfer to prepared casserole dish; sprinkle with cheese. Cover and bake in preheated oven about 45 minutes or until heated through and bubbling. Serve hot.

Meat Loaf Muffuletta Subs

Prep 15 minutes   **Bake** 30 minutes
Makes 6 servings

This Creole sandwich came to New Orleans by way of Sicily. My version swaps deli meat loaf and turkey for ham and salami. Pick up the meat, cheese, and rolls at the deli, then heat at home. My brother Johnny likes it the French Quarter way—with an ice-cold Barq's®.

1	jar (10-ounce) olive bruschetta, *Delallo*®
½	cup mayonnaise, *Hellmann's*® or *Best Foods*®
1	teaspoon Cajun seasoning, *McCormick*®
6	French rolls, split horizontally
½	pound thinly sliced cooked turkey breast
1½	pounds meat loaf from deli, sliced ¼ inch thick
12	slices thinly sliced provolone cheese (about 8 ounces)

1. Preheat oven to 325 degrees F. In a medium bowl, stir together olive bruschetta, mayonnaise, and Cajun seasoning. Generously spread mayonnaise mixture on both halves of French rolls. Top with turkey, meat loaf, and cheese to build sandwiches.

2. Wrap each sandwich in aluminum foil. Bake in preheated oven for 30 minutes. Serve warm.

Chinese Chicken Salad

Start to Finish 20 minutes
Makes 4 servings

1	quart deli coleslaw
1½	tablespoons Chinese chicken salad dressing mix, *Sun Bird*®
1	pound cooked breaded chicken pieces from deli, cut into bite-size chunks
1	cup chow mein noodles, *La Choy*®
1	can mandarin orange segments, drained, *Dole*®
2	scallions (green onions), sliced diagonally
¼	cup sliced almonds, *Planters*®

1. In a large bowl, stir together coleslaw and dry Chinese salad dressing mix. Toss together with chicken, chow mein noodles, mandarin oranges, and half of the scallions.

2. Divide among 4 chilled dinner plates. Sprinkle with remaining scallions and sliced almonds.

Barbecued Rib Hash

Start to Finish 25 minutes
Makes 8 servings

1	rack cooked barbecued spareribs from deli
¼	cup canola oil
4	cups Southern-style hash browns, *Ore-Ida*®
2½	cups frozen onions, *Ore-Ida*®
½	cup frozen chopped green bell peppers, *Pictsweet*®
1	can (11-ounce) mexicorn, drained, *Green Giant*®
1½	teaspoons Montreal steak seasoning, *McCormick*®
	Barbecue sauce, *Bull's-Eye*®

1. Remove meat from spareribs; chop meat. Set aside.

2. In a large skillet, heat oil over medium-high heat. Add potatoes, onions, and bell peppers in single layer. Fry for 7 to 8 minutes (without stirring).

3. Add rib meat, corn, and steak seasoning; turn with potatoes to combine. Cook 4 to 6 minutes more or until completely heated through. Serve immediately with barbecue sauce on the side.

TIP: For a more complete meal, serve with poached eggs.

Pasta with Sicilian Sauce

Start to Finish 25 minutes
Makes 8 servings

There are as many Sicilian sauces as there are *nonnis*, and my sauce, like most, is extra chunky. Chopping vegetables is a big time eater; the secret is to use salad bar veggies for fresh taste and superfast prep. Reduce the meat and this sauce pinch-hits as a pizza sauce.

1	pound fusilli or rotini pasta, *Barilla*®
2	tablespoons extra virgin olive oil, *Bertolli*®
1	pound spicy Italian sausage, casings removed
1	pound salad bar vegetables (such as onions, mushrooms, peas, olives, and/or artichokes)
1	jar (24-ounce) tomato basil marinara sauce, *Newman's Own*®
½	cup lower-sodium beef broth, *Swanson*®
½	teaspoon red pepper flakes, *McCormick*®
	Grated Parmesan cheese, *DiGiorno*®

1. In a large pot of boiling salted water, cook pasta following package directions. Drain and set aside.

2. In a large straight-sided skillet, heat oil over medium-high heat. Crumble sausage into skillet; cook until browned, stirring frequently to break up.

3. Add vegetables; cook for 4 to 5 minutes or until vegetables begin to soften. Stir in marinara sauce, broth, and red pepper flakes. Bring to a boil. Reduce heat. Simmer, uncovered, for 10 minutes.

4. Serve pasta topped with Sicilian Sauce and plenty of grated Parmesan.

Creole Chicken Noodle Casserole

Prep 20 minutes   **Bake** 45 minutes
Makes 6 servings

	Olive oil cooking spray, *Pam*®
8	ounces extra-wide egg noodles, *American Beauty*®
2	tablespoons canola oil
2	stalks celery, chopped
½	cup frozen chopped onions, *Ore-Ida*®
½	cup frozen chopped green bell peppers, *Pictsweet*®
1	teaspoon crushed garlic, *Gourmet Garden*®
1	can (10.75-ounce) condensed cream of celery soup, *Campbell's*®
1	cup evaporated milk, *Carnation*®
½	cup sour cream
2	teaspoons Cajun seasoning, *McCormick*®
1	cup chicken salad from deli
20	rich round crackers, crushed, *Ritz*®

1. Preheat oven to 350 degrees F. Lightly spray 2½-quart casserole dish with cooking spray; set aside.

2. Cook noodles according to package directions, except undercook by 1 to 2 minutes. Drain and set aside.

3. Meanwhile, in a medium skillet, heat oil over medium-high heat. Add celery; cook for 3 to 4 minutes or until celery begins to soften. Add onions, green peppers, and garlic; heat through. Set aside.

4. In a medium bowl, stir together celery soup, evaporated milk, sour cream, and Cajun seasoning. Fold in chicken salad and cooked vegetables. Carefully fold in cooked noodles. Transfer to prepared casserole dish. Sprinkle with crushed crackers. Bake in preheated oven for 45 minutes.

Chicken with Mole

Prep 25 minutes   **Bake** 30 minutes
Makes 4 servings

A Mexican mole is a chile-chocolate sauce. Making it from scratch is an all-day event, so shortcut it with a jar of mole sauce dolled up with pantry staples. Serve it over deli chicken with Mexican rice, tortillas, and avocado-dressed salad greens for a festive meal.

FOR MEXICAN RICE:

- 2 cups instant rice, *Uncle Ben's*®
- 1 can (14-ounce) reduced-sodium chicken broth, *Swanson*®
- 1 cup frozen seasoned vegetable blend, *Pictsweet*®
- 1 teaspoon paprika, *McCormick*®
- 1 teaspoon Mexican seasoning, *McCormick*®
- 1 can (10-ounce) diced tomatoes with chiles, drained, *Ro-Tel*®

FOR CHICKEN WITH MOLE:

- 1 can (14-ounce) reduced-sodium chicken broth, *Swanson*®
- ½ cup mole sauce, *Doña Maria*® *Original*
- ½ teaspoon ground cinnamon
- 1½ pounds fried chicken from deli
  Pickled whole hot peppers (optional)

1. Preheat oven to 350 degrees F. For Mexican Rice, in a medium saucepan, combine rice, broth, frozen vegetables, paprika, and Mexican seasoning. Bring to a boil. Cover and remove from heat. Let stand for 7 minutes. Stir in drained tomatoes. Transfer to 9×13-inch baking dish. Set aside.

2. For Chicken with Mole, rinse saucepan. In saucepan, combine broth, mole, and cinnamon. Cook for 6 to 8 minutes or until simmering, whisking until smooth and thickened.

3. Place fried chicken on rice; spoon mole mixture over chicken. Cover and bake for 30 to 35 minutes or until chicken is heated through. Garnish each serving with pickled peppers (optional).

Real-Quick Rotisserie Chicken

1. **Multitask with marinade.** Brush a pepper-spiked or citrus marinade inside and outside the skin and heat in the oven about 10 minutes. It'll moisten and flavor the chicken in one step.

2. **Serve different dippers.** Use mango salsa, peach chutney, and other mixtures as dipping sauces to give the chicken fun flavors.

3. **Buy two.** An average two-pound cooked chicken yields 3 to 3½ cups of meat. Enjoy it with vegetables one night, add it to canned soup the next, then store the leftovers.

4. **Eat the chicken within two hours.** If you're not going to serve it right away, pull the meat from the bones and refrigerate it in a shallow container. The chicken can be refrigerated for four days or frozen for up to four months.

5. **Take stock.** Remove the meat and toss the skin and bones into a simmering pot of packaged broth to make it doubly rich. Freeze in ice cube trays, then store cubes in zippered freezer bags.

The Recipes

Chicken Lasagna Roll-Ups

Prep 30 minutes **Bake** 45 minutes
Makes 6 servings

12	lasagna noodles, *Barilla*®
1	container (15-ounce) ricotta cheese, *Precious*®
1	egg, lightly beaten
1	tablespoon Italian seasoning, *McCormick*®
1	tablespoon crushed garlic, *Gourmet Garden*®
1	tablespoon chopped fresh parsley
1	jar (24-ounce) marinara sauce, *Newman's Own*®
2	cups shredded rotisserie chicken
2	cups shredded mozzarella cheese, *Sargento*®
2	tablespoons shredded Parmesan cheese, *DiGiorno*®

1. Preheat oven to 350 degrees F. In a large pot of boiling salted water, cook lasagna noodles for 8 minutes. Drain and rinse with cold water to stop cooking; drain again. Set aside.

2. In a medium bowl, stir together ricotta cheese, beaten egg, Italian seasoning, garlic, and parsley.

3. Spread ½ cup of the marinara sauce in a 9×13-inch baking dish. Spread each lasagna noodle with 2 tablespoons of the ricotta cheese mixture; sprinkle each with a scant 3 tablespoons of the shredded chicken and 2 heaping tablespoons of the mozzarella cheese. Roll up filled noodles and place, seam sides down, in prepared baking dish. Spoon the remaining marinara sauce over roll-ups.

4. Cover with foil. Bake in preheated oven for 35 minutes. Remove foil; sprinkle with Parmesan cheese. Bake for 10 minutes more. Serve hot.

Creamy Chicken Primavera Bake

Prep 20 minutes   **Bake** 45 minutes
Makes 6 servings

8	ounces rotini pasta, *Barilla®*
1	bag (16-ounce) frozen Italian-blend vegetables, *Birds Eye®*
1	jar (16-ounce) Alfredo sauce, *Classico®*
1	tablespoon Italian seasoning, *McCormick®*
1	teaspoon garlic salt, *Lawry's®*
1	rotisserie chicken, meat removed from bones and cut into 1-inch pieces
2	cups shredded mozzarella cheese, *Sargento®*
½	cup shredded Parmesan cheese, *DiGiorno®*

1. Preheat oven to 375 degrees F. In a large pot of boiling water, cook pasta for 7 minutes. Drain and set aside.

2. Meanwhile, in a covered microwave-safe dish, microwave vegetables on high setting (100 percent power) for 6 minutes. Drain well.

3. In a large bowl, stir together Alfredo sauce, Italian seasoning, and garlic salt. Add pasta, vegetables, chicken, and mozzarella cheese; fold to combine.

4. Transfer to a 3-quart casserole dish; sprinkle with Parmesan cheese. Cover and bake in preheated oven for 45 to 50 minutes or until heated through and bubbling.

Chicken Cassoulet

Prep 25 minutes   **Bake** 50 minutes
Makes 8 servings

In France this hearty dish is made by tossing leftover meats in a stew with beans and spices, and you can do the same. With chicken, sausage, and bacon, it's a protein-packed meal. Serve it with a light salad and fruit for dessert.

½	pound pork sausage with sage, *Jimmy Dean*®
1	whole rotisserie chicken, meat removed from bones and shredded
2	cans (15 ounces each) cannellini beans, drained, *Progresso*®
1	can (15-ounce) diced tomatoes, drained, *Hunt's*®
1	cup frozen seasoned vegetables, *Pictsweet*®
1	tablespoon herbes de Provence, *McCormick*®
2	teaspoons crushed garlic, *Gourmet Garden*®
1	cup white wine
1	can (14.5-ounce) reduced-sodium chicken broth, *Swanson*®
1	cup bread crumbs, *Progresso*®
¼	cup real bacon pieces, *Hormel*®
½	stick (¼ cup) butter, melted

1. Preheat oven to 375 degrees F. Form sausage into 1-inch-thick patties. In a medium skillet, cook sausage until browned. Place on paper towels to drain.

2. In a large bowl, combine chicken, beans, tomatoes, frozen vegetables, herbes, and garlic. Crumble cooked sausage; fold sausage into chicken mixture. Transfer to 2½-quart casserole dish. Pour in wine and broth.

3. In a small bowl, stir together bread crumbs, bacon pieces, and melted butter. Sprinkle over cassoulet.

4. Bake in preheated oven for 50 to 60 minutes. Using the back of a large spoon, press bread crumb mixture into cassoulet every 20 minutes. Serve hot.

Fiesta Chicken and Rice

Prep 30 minutes   **Bake** 30 minutes
Makes 6 servings

2	packages (5 ounces each) saffron rice, *Mahatma*®
3⅓	cups reduced-sodium chicken broth, *Swanson*®
1	can (15-ounce) reduced-sodium black beans, drained, *S&W*®
1	jar (2-ounce) chopped pimiento, *Dromedary*®
1	rotisserie chicken, removed from bones and cut into 2-inch pieces
2	cups frozen bell pepper strips, thawed, *Birds Eye*®
1	cup chunky salsa, *Newman's Own*®
1	tablespoon frozen orange juice concentrate, *Minute Maid*®
	Sliced jalapeño peppers (optional) (see note, page 77)

1. Preheat oven to 375 degrees F. In a medium saucepan, combine rice and broth; cook following package directions. When cooked, stir in black beans and pimiento. Spread in a 9×13-inch baking dish; set aside.

2. In a large bowl, toss together chicken and pepper strips. Spoon chicken mixture over rice mixture in baking dish.

3. In a small bowl, stir together salsa and orange juice concentrate. Spoon over chicken mixture. Cover and bake in preheated oven for 30 to 40 minutes or until heated through. Garnish with sliced jalapeño peppers (optional).

Chicken and Sweet Potato Gumbo

Prep 25 minutes   **Cook** 30 minutes
Makes 6 to 8 servings

1	package (12-ounce) Cajun-style andouille, cut into rounds, *Aidells®*
2	tablespoons canola oil
½	cups frozen chopped onions, *Ore-Ida®*
1	package (16-ounce) frozen cut okra, *Pictsweet®*
2	stalks celery, diced
½	cup frozen chopped green bell pepper, *Pictsweet®*
3	cans (14 ounces each) reduced-sodium chicken broth, *Swanson®*
1	box (4.5-ounce) gumbo base, *Zatarain's®*
1	whole rotisserie chicken, meat removed from bones and chopped
1	can (29-ounce) sweet potatoes, *Princella®*
2	tablespoons *Old Bay®* seasoning
	Hot cooked rice

1. In a Dutch oven, brown andouille rounds over medium-high heat. Remove and set aside.

2. Add oil to Dutch oven and heat. Add onions, okra, celery, and bell pepper. Cook for 3 to 4 minutes or until celery is tender. Add broth and gumbo base; bring to a boil. Stir in andouille, chicken, sweet potatoes, and seasoning. Cover and simmer for 30 minutes.

3. Serve over hot cooked rice.

Speedy Smothered Chicken

Prep 15 minutes   **Bake** 45 minutes
Makes 4 servings

1	rotisserie chicken, cut into 8 pieces
1	package (8-ounce) sliced fresh mushrooms
1	large yellow onion, sliced
1	can (10.75-ounce) condensed cream of mushroom and garlic soup, *Campbell's*®
1	can (10-ounce) white sauce, *Aunt Penny's*®
2	tablespoons lemon juice, *Minute Maid*®
1	teaspoon crushed garlic, *Gourmet Garden*®

1. Preheat oven to 375 degrees F. Place chicken pieces, skin sides up, in a 9×13-inch baking pan. Cover chicken with sliced mushrooms and sliced onion; set aside.

2. In a medium bowl, stir together cream of mushroom and garlic soup, white sauce, lemon juice, and garlic. Cover with aluminum foil and bake in preheated oven for 45 minutes.

Chicken Tikka Masala

Prep 25 minutes   **Cook** 10 minutes
Makes 6 servings

1	rotisserie chicken, meat removed from bones and cut into 2-inch pieces
1	tablespoon garam masala, *McCormick*®
2	teaspoons paprika, *McCormick*®
2	teaspoons ground cumin, *McCormick*®
2	tablespoons canola oil
1	fresh jalapeño chile, seeded and chopped*
2	tablespoons crushed garlic, *Gourmet Garden*®
1	tablespoon minced ginger, *Gourmet Garden*®
1	can (10.75-ounce) condensed tomato soup, *Campbell's*®
1	cup half-and-half or light cream
¼	cup chopped fresh cilantro
	Hot cooked rice
	Fresh cilantro leaves (optional)

1. In a large bowl, toss chicken pieces with garam masala, paprika, and cumin; set aside. In a large skillet, heat oil over medium-high heat. Add jalapeño; cook for 1 minute. Add chicken, garlic, and ginger; cook about 2 minutes more or until fragrant.

2. Add tomato soup and half-and-half, stirring until combined. Cook on low heat for 10 minutes. Stir in cilantro. Serve over hot cooked rice. Garnish with fresh cilantro (optional).

***NOTE:** Because chiles contain volatile oils that can burn your skin and eyes, avoid direct contact with them if possible. Wear plastic gloves. If your bare hands do touch the chiles, wash your hands with warm soapy water.

Island Chicken Pizza

Start to Finish 30 minutes
Makes 4 servings

My brother Rich loves to grill. In cooler months he re-creates this good mood food with a rotisserie chicken. The tropical flavors evoke the easy appeal of the Caribbean—and the prepwork is equally laid-back, thanks to canned fruit and packaged jerk spices.

	Nonstick cooking spray, *Pam*®
¾	cup chili sauce, *Heinz*®
1	cup refrigerated tropical fruit, *Dole*®
2	teaspoons Jamaican jerk seasoning, *McCormick*®
2	teaspoons minced ginger, *Gourmet Garden*®
1	can (13.8-ounce) refrigerated pizza crust, *Pillsbury*®
3	cups shredded Jack cheese, *Sargento*®
2	cups shredded rotisserie chicken
1	tablespoon chopped fresh cilantro
	Fresh cilantro sprig (optional)
	Crushed red pepper (optional)

1. Preheat oven to 400 degrees F. Spray baking sheet with cooking spray; set aside.

2. In a small bowl, stir together chili sauce, ¼ cup juice from tropical fruit jar, jerk seasoning, and ginger; set aside.

3. Press out pizza dough on prepared baking sheet into a 12-inch square. Bake in preheated oven for 8 minutes.

4. Remove crust from oven and spread sauce mixture over, leaving a 1-inch border. Top with cheese, fruit, chicken, and cilantro. Bake for 14 to 18 minutes or until cheese is melted and beginning to bubble. Garnish with cilantro sprig and serve with crushed red pepper (optional). Serve hot.

Mediterranean Chicken Gyros

Start to Finish 20 minutes
Makes 6 servings

Gyros are Greek fast food, and my version makes them even faster by rolling rotisserie chicken in a ready-made pita.

2	cups sliced rotisserie chicken
2	tablespoons lemon juice, *Minute Maid®*
1	tablespoon Greek seasoning, *Spice Islands®*
½	teaspoon paprika
½	cup chopped, seeded cucumber
¼	cup chopped red onion
2	teaspoons fresh mint leaves
1	cup fat-free plain yogurt, *Dannon®*
6	pita bread rounds, *Sara Lee®*
3	cups spring salad mix, *Fresh Express®*
	Lemon slices (optional)

1. In a medium bowl, toss together chicken, lemon juice, Greek seasoning, and paprika; set aside. In a small bowl, stir chopped cucumber, red onion, and mint into yogurt.

2. Cut pita bread in half and open pocket. Stuff with salad mix and chicken mixture; serve with spoonfuls of the yogurt mixture. Serve with lemon slices (optional).

Chicken Chopped Cobb

Start to Finish 20 minutes
Makes 4 servings

FOR COBB DRESSING:

½	cup olive oil and vinegar dressing, *Newman's Own®*
2	tablespoons ranch dressing mix, *Hidden Valley®*

FOR COBB SALAD:

10	cups romaine mix, chopped, *Fresh Express®*
2	cups shredded rotisserie chicken
⅓	cup crumbled blue cheese, *Sargento®*
4	hard-cooked eggs, peeled and sliced
2	plum tomatoes, cut into wedges
1	medium ripe avocado, diced
⅓	cup crumbled real bacon, *Hormel®*
4	scallions (green onions), thinly sliced

1. For Cobb Dressing, in a small bowl, whisk together oil and vinegar dressing and ranch dressing mix.

2. For Cobb Salad, divide chopped romaine among 4 salad bowls. Arrange shredded chicken, blue cheese, eggs, tomatoes, avocado, bacon, and scallions over the romaine. Garnish with sliced scallions. Serve Cobb Dressing in small ramekins on the side.

Warm Chicken and Potato Salad

Prep 15 minutes   **Roast** 20 minutes
Makes 8 servings

1	bag (16-ounce) precooked potatoes, *Reeser's*®
½	of a medium red onion, diced
1	tablespoon extra virgin olive oil, *Bertolli*®
½	cup sour cream
2	tablespoons Dijon mustard, *Grey Poupon*®
1	rotisserie chicken, meat removed from bones and shredded
¼	cup crumbled real bacon, *Hormel*®
¼	cup chopped sun-dried tomatoes
1	fresh jalapeño chile, seeded and finely chopped (see note, page 77)
1	tablespoon finely chopped fresh parsley
1	teaspoon fines herbes, *Spice Islands*®

1. Preheat oven to 450 degrees F. On a large baking sheet, toss together potatoes, red onion, and oil. Roast in preheated oven for 20 minutes.

2. Meanwhile, in a large bowl, stir together sour cream and mustard. Add chicken, bacon, tomatoes, jalapeño, parsley, and fines herbes. Add cooked potatoes and onion; fold together until combined.

Thai Chicken Salad

Start to Finish 20 minutes
Makes 4 servings

FOR PEANUT BUTTER DRESSING:

¼	cup red wine vinaigrette, *Wish-Bone*®
2	tablespoons creamy peanut butter, *Skippy*®
2	tablespoons water
1	tablespoon crushed garlic, *Gourmet Garden*®
1	tablespoon lime juice, *ReaLime*®
1	tablespoons chili garlic sauce, *Lee Kum Kee*®

FOR CHICKEN SALAD:

8	cups butter lettuce mix, *Fresh Express*®
2	cups shredded rotisserie chicken
1	cup seeded and diced cucumber
1½	cups sliced red, yellow, and/or green bell pepper
½	cup fresh cilantro leaves
¼	cup fresh mint leaves
½	cup fried rice noodles, *La Choy*®
½	cup cashews, roughly chopped, *Planters*®
	Lime wedges (optional)

1. For Peanut Butter Dressing, whisk together vinaigrette, peanut butter, the water, the garlic, lime juice, and chili garlic sauce; set aside.

2. For Chicken Salad, divide lettuce among 4 salad plates. In a medium bowl, toss together chicken, cucumber, red pepper, cilantro, and mint. Add Peanut Butter Dressing; gently toss to coat all ingredients. Spoon chicken mixture over lettuce on salad plates. Sprinkle with rice noodles and cashews. Serve with lime wedges (optional).

Fix It and Freeze It

1. Freeze smart. Separate appetizers, meatballs, cookies, or candy on a baking sheet, freeze solid, then transfer them to a container. Separate layers with parchment paper to prevent them from clumping together.

2. Bag broths and sauces. Freeze liquids flat in plastic bags, then stand them up sideways for storage. They'll take up less space and thaw faster.

3. Cool foods before freezing. Cooling food first speeds up the freezing process and reduces condensation. The faster food freezes, the fresher it tastes when thawed.

4. Cook when you can. Spend a Sunday afternoon cooking and freeze enough meals to eat all week. Freeze food in individual or meal-size portions—it'll thaw quicker and you can pop out the number of servings you need.

5. Pack food tightly. Squeeze excess air out of bags to prevent freezer burn. Fill containers full, leaving a little space at the top to prevent liquids from expanding and sticking to the lid.

The Recipes

Pecan-Crusted Orange Curry Chicken

Prep 20 minutes **Bake** 20 minutes (after thawing)
Makes 4 servings

A pecan crust makes this pretty dish taste like company's coming, though it's quick enough to serve any night for a family treat. Orange juice and cherries add a sweet-tart tang. Separate the chicken and coating for freezing, then assemble and bake to serve.

4	boneless, skinless chicken breasts, trimmed
1	teaspoon curry powder, *McCormick®*
1	tablespoon butter
2	tablespoons frozen orange juice concentrate, *Minute Maid®*
½	cup mayonnaise, *Hellmann's®* or *Best Foods®*
½	teaspoon salt
1	cup panko (Japanese-style) bread crumbs, *Ian's®*
½	cup pecans, finely chopped, *Diamond®*
¼	cup dried cherries, finely chopped, *Mariani®*
2	tablespoons canola oil
	Nonstick cooking spray, *Pam®*

1. Rinse chicken with cold water and pat dry with paper towels. Place chicken in a large zip-top plastic bag; set aside. In a dry skillet, heat curry powder over medium heat until curry just becomes fragrant; add butter. When butter has melted, remove from heat and stir in orange juice concentrate. Transfer orange juice mixture to a small bowl. When cooled, stir in mayonnaise and salt. Pour curry mixture over chicken in plastic bag. Squeeze out air and seal.

2. In small bowl, combine panko bread crumbs, pecans, dried cherries, and oil; mix well. Transfer bread crumb mixture to a small zip-top plastic bag; squeeze out air and seal. Place sealed bag with chicken and sealed bag with bread crumbs in large freezer bag; seal and freeze.

THAWING AND COOKING: Thaw chicken breasts completely in refrigerator. Preheat oven to 375 degrees F. Empty bread crumb mixture onto a plate. Press chicken breasts into bread crumbs to coat. Place on a baking sheet that has been lightly sprayed with cooking spray. Bake in preheated oven for about 20 minutes or until an instant-read thermometer inserted in center of chicken breast registers 170 degrees F.

Raspberry Mustard-Crusted Chicken

Prep 15 minutes   **Bake** 20 minutes (after thawing)
Makes 4 servings

4	boneless, skinless chicken breasts, trimmed
¼	cup Dijon mustard, *Grey Poupon®*
¼	cup frozen raspberries, thawed, *Dole®*
2	tablespoons raspberry preserves, *Smucker's®*
½	cup panko (Japanese-style) bread crumbs, *Ian's®*
½	cup pecans, finely chopped, *Diamond®*
1	tablespoon dried parsley, *McCormick®*
½	teaspoon salt
½	teaspoon freshly ground black pepper
	Nonstick cooking spray, *Pam®*
	Fresh chopped parsley (optional)

1. Place chicken in a large zip-top plastic bag; set aside. In a small bowl, stir together mustard, thawed raspberries, and preserves. Pour into bag with chicken. Massage bag gently to coat chicken. Squeeze air from bag and seal. Set aside.

2. In a small zip-top plastic bag, combine bread crumbs, finely chopped pecans, parsley, salt, and pepper. Shake to combine. Squeeze air from bag and seal. Place sealed bag with chicken and sealed bag with bread crumbs in another large freezer bag. Seal bag, label, and freeze.

THAWING AND COOKING: Thaw chicken completely in refrigerator. Preheat oven to 375 degrees F. Empty bread crumb mixture onto a plate. Press chicken breasts into bread crumbs to coat. Place chicken on a baking sheet that has been lightly sprayed with cooking spray. Bake in preheated oven about 20 minutes or until an instant-read thermometer inserted in center of chicken breast registers 170 degrees F. Sprinkle with chopped parsley (optional).

Tarragon Turkey and Rice

Prep 15 minutes **Bake** 35 minutes
Stand 30 minutes **Reheat** 25 minutes
Makes 4 servings

For versatility and taste, turkey tenderloins can't be beat. Cooking the companion rice in mushroom soup and chicken broth intensifies the flavor. Low-fat poultry freezes superbly, so pack single servings in microwavable containers and take one to the office for lunch.

1 can (10.75-ounce) condensed cream of mushroom soup, *Campbell's*®
1 cup reduced-sodium chicken broth, *Swanson*®
1 box (5.9-ounce) garlic and herb long grain and wild
   rice mix, *Near East*®
1 tablespoon lemon juice, *Minute Maid*®
1 teaspoon crushed garlic, *Gourmet Garden*®
1 tablespoon dried tarragon, *McCormick*®
1½ teaspoons garlic salt, *Lawry's*®
1¼ pounds turkey breast tenderloin, cut into serving-size portions
   Fresh tarragon sprig (optional)

1. Preheat oven to 350 degrees F. In a medium bowl, stir together mushroom soup, broth, rice mix, lemon juice, and garlic. Transfer to 9×13-inch baking dish; set aside.

2. Combine tarragon and garlic salt. Sprinkle tarragon mixture over all sides of the turkey portions and place on top of the rice mixture. Cover and bake in the preheated oven for 45 minutes.

3. Serve hot or prepare to freeze. If freezing, cool on a wire rack for 20 to 25 minutes. Cover loosely with aluminum foil and cool completely in refrigerator. Once cool, remove foil, wrap tightly with plastic wrap, and overwrap with aluminum foil. Label and freeze.

THAWING AND REHEATING: Thaw completely in refrigerator. Preheat oven to 350 degrees F. Remove plastic wrap and re-cover with foil. Let stand at room temperature for 30 minutes. Bake in preheated oven for 25 to 30 minutes or until heated through. Garnish with a tarragon sprig (optional).

Mom's Bacon-Wrapped Meat Loaves

Prep 15 minutes   **Bake** 35 minutes
Stand 30 minutes   **Reheat** 20 minutes
Makes 6 servings (3 loaves)

9	slices bacon
¾	pound lean ground beef
¾	pound ground pork
¾	pound ground veal
1	egg
¼	cup chili sauce, *Heinz*®
½	cup rolled oats, *Quaker*®
½	cup frozen chopped onions, *Ore-Ida*®
2	teaspoons crushed garlic, *Gourmet Garden*®
1	packet (1-ounce) beefy onion soup mix, *Lipton*®

1. Preheat oven to 375 degrees F. Poke holes in the bottom of three 5⅝×3³⁄₁₆-inch disposable foil loaf pans. Line each pan with 3 slices bacon lengthwise; set aside.

2. In a large bowl, combine ground beef, ground pork, ground veal, egg, and chili sauce; mix well. Add rolled oats, onions, garlic, and dry soup mix; mix well. Spoon meat mixture evenly among bacon-lined pans and smooth the top.

3. Place pan on a wire rack over a foil-lined baking sheet. Bake in preheated oven for 35 to 40 minutes or until instant-read thermometer inserted in center registers 160 degrees F.*

4. Slice and serve hot or prepare to freeze. If freezing, cool on wire rack for 20 to 25 minutes. Place each meat loaf and pan in another foil pan and cover loosely with aluminum foil. Cool completely in refrigerator. Once cooled, remove foil and wrap each loaf in pan tightly with plastic wrap. Overwrap with aluminum foil. Label and freeze.

THAWING AND REHEATING: Thaw meat loaf completely in refrigerator. Preheat oven to 350 degrees F. Remove plastic wrap and re-cover with foil. Allow meat loaf to stand at room temperature for 30 minutes. Bake in preheated oven for 20 to 25 minutes or until heated through.

*NOTE: To crisp bacon on meat loaves, after reheating, preheat broiler. Invert hot meat loaves onto a foil-lined baking pan. Broil for 2 minutes or until bacon is crisp.

Meatballs and Tomato Gravy

Prep 25 minutes   **Cook** 15 minutes plus reheating
Makes 4 servings

FOR TOMATO GRAVY:

1	jar (24-ounce) marinara sauce, *Newman's Own*®
½	cup red wine
½	cup reduced-sodium beef broth, *Swanson*®
2	teaspoons dried oregano, *McCormick*®
2	teaspoons crushed garlic, *Gourmet Garden*®

FOR PARMESAN MEATBALLS:

½	cup Italian bread crumbs, *Progresso*®
⅓	cup evaporated milk, *Carnation*®
1	pound ground beef
¼	cup grated Parmesan cheese, *DiGiorno*®
1	tablespoon Italian seasoning, *McCormick*®
¾	teaspoon salt
½	teaspoon black pepper
	Hot cooked pasta
	Grated Parmesan cheese (optional)

1. For Tomato Gravy, in a large straight-side skillet, combine marinara, wine, broth, oregano, and garlic. Simmer, uncovered, on low to medium heat while you prepare meatballs.

2. For Parmesan Meatballs, in a large bowl, combine bread crumbs and milk; soak for 5 minutes. Add ground beef, Parmesan cheese, Italian seasoning, salt, and pepper; mix well. Wet your hands to keep mixture from sticking to them and roll into 1½-inch meatballs (you should have about 30).

3. Raise heat under sauce to medium. When sauce is almost boiling, carefully drop meatballs into sauce. Cover and cook for 10 minutes. Remove lid. Simmer for 5 minutes more.

4. Serve over hot cooked pasta or prepare to freeze. If freezing, cool for 20 to 25 minutes. Transfer to freezer container and cover loosely with aluminum foil. Cool completely in refrigerator. Once cool, remove foil; cover tightly. Label and freeze.

THAWING AND REHEATING: Thaw meatballs completely in refrigerator. Transfer to a large skillet and bring to a boil. If necessary, thin sauce with beef broth. Serve with hot cooked pasta. Sprinkle with grated Parmesan cheese (optional).

Beefy Braised Short Ribs

Prep 25 minutes
Cook 8 to 10 hours in slow cooker plus reheating
Makes 6 servings

2	red onions, sliced
5	pounds beef short ribs
1	tablespoon Montreal steak seasoning, *McCormick® Grill Mates*
2	tablespoons canola oil
2	cups lower-sodium beef broth, *Swanson®*
1	cup Merlot or other red wine
1	package (0.6-ounce) au jus gravy mix, *Knorr®*

1. Place red onion in a 5-quart slow cooker. Season short ribs with steak seasoning. In a large skillet, heat oil over medium-high heat. Working in batches, brown ribs on all sides and transfer to slow cooker. Stir together broth, wine, and au jus gravy mix. Pour over short ribs. Cover; cook on low-heat setting for 8 to 10 hours. Serve hot or prepare to freeze. If freezing, cool completely, cover, and refrigerate overnight. Remove from refrigerator; discard fat layer from the top. Transfer to an airtight container, cover, and freeze.

THAWING AND REHEATING: Thaw completely in refrigerator. Transfer to Dutch oven and simmer over medium heat until heated through.

Ranchero Beef

Prep 25 minutes   **Cook** 1 hour 10 minutes plus reheating
Makes 6 servings

2	tablespoons extra virgin olive oil, *Bertolli®*
1¼	pounds beef stew meat, cut into bite-size pieces
2	tablespoons Mexican seasoning, *McCormick®*
2	teaspoons Montreal steak seasoning, *McCormick® Grill Mates®*
1	jar (16-ounce) chunky salsa, *Newman's Own®*
1	bag (14-ounce) frozen pearl onions, *C&W®*
1	can (11-ounce) mexicorn, *Green Giant®*
1	can (4-ounce) diced green chiles, *Ortega®*
½	cup lower-sodium beef broth, *Swanson®*
½	cup gold tequila, *Jose Cuervo®*
2	teaspoons crushed garlic, *Gourmet Garden®*
¼	cup chopped fresh cilantro

1. In a large pot or Dutch oven, heat oil over high heat. Season beef with Mexican seasoning and steak seasoning. Working in batches if necessary, add meat to hot oil; brown meat on all sides. Add salsa, pearl onions, mexicorn, chiles, broth, tequila, and garlic. Bring to a boil; reduce to low simmer. Cover and simmer for 1 to 1½ hours or until beef is tender. Remove lid and simmer for 10 to 15 minutes more until liquid thickens.

2. Remove from heat and stir in cilantro. Serve hot or prepare to freeze. If freezing, cool on a wire rack for 20 to 25 minutes. Transfer to freezer container and cover loosely with aluminum foil. Cool completely in refrigerator. Once cool, cover tightly. Label and freeze.

THAWING AND REHEATING: Thaw Ranchero Beef completely in refrigerator. Transfer to a large pot and bring to a boil over medium heat, stirring occasionally.

Pork Chops and Apples

Prep 15 minutes **Bake** 40 minutes (after thawing)
Makes 6 servings

6	thick-cut pork chops
½	cup refrigerated egg product, *Egg Beaters*®
2½	teaspoons pumpkin pie spice, *McCormick*®
1	teaspoon garlic salt, *Lawry's*®
1	teaspoon dried whole leaf sage
¼	cup packed brown sugar, *C&H*®
2	tablespoons butter, softened
2	packages (14 ounces each) presliced apples, *Chiquita*®
1	cup panko (Japanese-style) bread crumbs, *Ian's*®
	Fresh snipped parsley (optional)

1. Place chops in a large zip-top plastic bag; set aside. In a small bowl, whisk together egg product, ½ teaspoon of the pumpkin pie spice, the garlic salt, and sage. Pour egg product mixture over chops in bag. Massage bag to coat chops. Squeeze out air and seal.

2. In a small bowl, stir together brown sugar, butter, and the remaining 2 teaspoons pumpkin pie spice. Add apples; toss to coat. Place apple mixture in a large zip-top plastic bag. Place sealed bag of chops and sealed bag of apples in large freezer bag. Seal bag, label, and freeze.

THAWING AND COOKING: Thaw completely in refrigerator. Preheat oven to 375 degrees F. Place apples in 9×13-inch baking pan; set aside. Remove chops from egg mixture. Place bread crumbs in shallow dish; coat chops with bread crumbs. Place chops on top of apples. Bake for 40 to 45 minutes. Sprinkle with snipped parsley (optional).

Sherried Pork Fillets

Prep 20 minutes   **Fry** 4 minutes per batch (after thawing)
Makes 4 servings

Instead of the usual sherried cream sauce, my rendition goes more piquant, pairing sweet maple syrup with sharp Dijon mustard and smoky bacon in an olive oil base. Freeze the pork and bacon in separate bags.

1¼	pounds pork tenderloin, trimmed
1	cup dry sherry, *Christian Brothers*®
2	tablespoons pure maple syrup, *Spring Tree*®
1	tablespoon fine herbes, *Spice Islands*®
2	teaspoons Dijon mustard, *Grey Poupon*®
2	tablespoons extra virgin olive oil, *Bertolli*®
4	slices bacon, chopped
½	cup reduced-sodium chicken broth, *Swanson*®
½	cup all-purpose flour

1. Slice trimmed tenderloin into 1-inch-thick pieces. Place each pork piece between 2 sheets of plastic wrap. Using flat side of a meat mallet, pound pork until ¼ inch thick.

2. Place pork in a large zip-top plastic bag and set aside. In a small bowl, whisk together ½ cup of the sherry, the syrup, fine herbes, and mustard; continue whisking while drizzling in oil. Pour sherry-oil mixture over pork in bag. Squeeze out air and seal.

3. Place chopped bacon in a small zip-top plastic bag and remaining ½ cup sherry and the broth in another small zip-top plastic bag. Squeeze air out of bags and seal both bags. Place all 3 sealed bags in large freezer bag. Seal bag, label, and freeze.

THAWING AND COOKING: Thaw pork fillets completely in refrigerator. In a large skillet, cook chopped bacon to render fat and just until crispy. Remove bacon with slotted spoon and place on paper towels to drain. Remove pork from marinade; discard marinade. Dredge pork in flour. Working in batches, fry pork in rendered bacon fat over medium heat for 4 to 6 minutes or until golden brown, turning once. Deglaze skillet with remaining ½ cup sherry and the broth, scraping up brown bits. Strain and return to skillet; bring to simmer. Add pork and bacon and coat with sauce.

French Pork Casserole

Prep 25 minutes **Bake** 30 minutes
Stand 30 minutes **Reheat** 25 minutes
Makes 4 servings

	Nonstick cooking spray, *Pam®*
1	bag (16-ounce) precooked rosemary potatoes, *Reeser's®*
2	tablespoons canola oil
1	pound pork tenderloin, trimmed and cut into bite-size pieces
1	cup chopped sweet onion
1	can (14-ounce) diced tomatoes, *Hunt's®*
¼	cup crumbled real bacon, *Hormel®*
¼	cup cognac
2	teaspoons herbes de Provence, *McCormick®*
1	teaspoon salt
½	teaspoon freshly ground black pepper
1	can (10-ounce) white sauce, *Aunt Penny's®*
15	buttery crackers, crushed, *Ritz®*
	Fresh rosemary sprigs (optional)

1. Preheat oven to 350 degrees F. Lightly spray a 2½-quart casserole dish with cooking spray. Place potatoes in casserole; set aside.

2. In a Dutch oven, heat oil over medium-high heat. Add pork to hot oil; brown on all sides. Once pork is browned, add onion and cook for 2 minutes. Add tomatoes, bacon, cognac, and herbes. Season with salt and pepper. Bring to a boil. Remove from heat and stir in white sauce. Transfer to the casserole dish. Top with crushed crackers. Bake in preheated oven about 30 minutes or until bubbling.

3. Serve hot or prepare to freeze. If freezing, cool on a wire rack for 20 to 25 minutes. Cover loosely with aluminum foil and cool completely in refrigerator. Once cool, remove foil, wrap tightly with plastic wrap, and overwrap with aluminum foil. Label and freeze.

THAWING AND REHEATING: Thaw completely in refrigerator. Preheat oven to 350 degrees F. Remove plastic wrap and re-cover with foil. Let stand at room temperature for 30 minutes. Bake in preheated oven for 25 to 30 minutes or until heated through. Garnish with rosemary sprigs (optional).

Veal Croquettes

Prep 20 minutes   **Cook** 8 minutes per batch
Reheat 20 minutes   **Makes** 8 servings

1   bag (half of a 12-ounce box) seasoned bread dressing mix,
       Mrs. Cubbison's®
1   cup evaporated milk, *Carnation*®
1   packet (1.6-ounce) garlic and herb sauce mix, *Knorr*®
2   pounds ground veal
1   egg, lightly beaten
      Canola oil
      Purchased marinara sauce, warmed (optional)

1. Empty dressing mix into a large zip-top plastic bag. Squeeze air out of bag and seal. Using a rolling pin, crush dressing mix into a fine crumb. Measure ½ cup of the bread crumbs and place in a small bowl. Add evaporated milk and sauce mix to the bowl of bread crumbs; set aside to soak. Place the remaining bread crumbs on a plate and set aside.

2. In a large bowl, combine ground veal and egg; add soaked bread crumbs and milk. Using clean hands or a wooden spoon, thoroughly mix veal mixture. Shape into 3×1½-inch croquettes. Roll croquettes in bread crumbs.

3. Pour enough oil into a large skillet to cover the bottom. Heat oil over medium heat. Working in batches, fry croquettes in hot oil for 8 to 10 minutes or until golden brown and cooked through; do not overcrowd pan.

4. Serve immediately or prepare to freeze. If freezing, cool croquettes on a baking sheet and refrigerate for 1 hour. Place baking sheet in freezer for 3 to 4 hours or until completely frozen. Transfer croquettes to a freezer container and freeze for up to 3 months.

THAWING AND REHEATING: Thaw overnight in the refrigerator. Preheat oven to 350 degrees F. Place croquettes in a 9×13-inch baking pan. Bake in preheated oven for 20 to 25 minutes or until heated through. Serve with warm marinara sauce (optional).

Creamy Spinach Ricotta Pasta

Prep 20 minutes
Stand 30 minutes
Makes 8 servings
Bake 20 minutes
Reheat: 25 minutes

	Nonstick cooking spray, *Pam®*
1	pound rigatoni pasta, *Barilla®*
1	can (15-ounce) diced tomatoes with basil, onions, and garlic, undrained, *Hunt's®*
1	cup frozen chopped onions, *Ore-Ida®*
1	box (10-ounce) frozen chopped spinach, *Birds Eye®*
2½	cups Alfredo sauce, *Classico®*
1½	cups ricotta cheese, *Precious®*
1	teaspoon garlic salt, *Lawry's®*
½	teaspoon black pepper
⅓	cup Italian bread crumbs, *Progresso®*
¼	cup grated Parmesan cheese, *DiGiorno®*
1	tablespoon extra virgin olive oil, *Bertolli®*

1. Preheat oven to 425 degrees F. Lightly spray 9×13-inch baking dish with cooking spray; set aside.

2. In a large pot of boiling salted water, cook pasta following package directions. Drain and return to pot. Add undrained tomatoes and onions and toss to combine; set aside.

3. Cook spinach in microwave following package directions. When cool enough to handle, squeeze out excess moisture. Transfer to a medium bowl. Add Alfredo sauce, ricotta cheese, garlic salt, and pepper; stir to combine. Transfer to pot with pasta; toss to combine. Transfer to prepared baking pan. Set aside.

4. Mix together bread crumbs, Parmesan cheese, and oil. Sprinkle over pasta. Bake in preheated oven for 20 to 25 minutes or until golden brown and bubbling.

5. Serve hot or prepare to freeze. If freezing, cool on a wire rack for 20 to 25 minutes. Cover loosely with aluminum foil and cool completely in refrigerator. Once cool, remove foil, wrap tightly with plastic wrap, and overwrap with aluminum foil. Label and freeze.

THAWING AND REHEATING: Thaw completely in refrigerator. Preheat oven to 350 degrees F. Remove plastic wrap and re-cover with foil. Let pasta stand at room temperature for 30 minutes. Bake in preheated oven for 25 to 30 minutes or until heated through.

Cook Once, Eat Thrice

1. Divide and conquer. When you're cooking for multiple meals, divide the portions before serving; serve one and refrigerate the rest. This keeps carryovers from becoming pickedovers.

2. Remake leftovers the easy way. Instead of making a different meal the next day, simplify dinner by using leftover meat in a sandwich. Make a quick mixture of mayonnaise, red onion, and sweet pickle relish to spread on the bread.

3. Master the casserole. Do as the French do—toss your leftover meats and some fresh vegetables into a dish with spices and wine for a one-dish dinner that's easy to clean up.

4. Cook pasta by the potful. Toss warm pasta with a spoonful of vegetable oil to keep the strands from sticking together, let cool, then seal any extra in a zip-top bag. The next day you'll have a ready-made side dish!

5. Make some dough. Frozen puff pastry is a simple way to give leftover entrées gourmet appeal. Just roll, bake, and serve alongside leftover soups, stews, and casseroles.

The Recipes

Herb Butter-Roasted Turkey

Prep 30 minutes   **Roast** 4 hours
Chill 15 minutes   **Makes** 12 servings

Turkey's lean protein is so healthy, you'll want to eat turkey every night. Roast it with herbs for Sunday dinner, then simmer with peppercorns and sage dumplings for a savory stew. Go for three by creaming it with cheese, butter, and bacon in an open-face Mornay.

MEAL 1

1½	sticks (¾ cup) butter, softened
2	tablespoons garlic herb sauce mix, *Knorr®*
1½	teaspoons poultry seasoning, *McCormick®*
1½	teaspoons crushed garlic, *Gourmet Garden®*
1	bag (32-ounce) celery and carrot party sticks, *Ready Pac®*
2	large onions, diced
1	container (32-ounce) reduced-sodium chicken broth, *Swanson®*
12	pounds whole turkey, thawed if frozen
1	tablespoon salt
1	tablespoon ground black pepper, *McCormick®*
3	packets (0.75 ounce each) fresh poultry herb blend (sage, thyme, and rosemary), *Herb Thyme®*
1	lemon, thickly sliced

1. In a small bowl, combine softened butter, garlic herb sauce mix, poultry seasoning, and crushed garlic. Use a fork to stir together until well mixed. Cover and refrigerate for 15 to 30 minutes or until butter mixture is firm but not hard.

2. Preheat the oven to 450 degrees F. In the bottom of a roasting pan, arrange celery and carrot party sticks and half of the diced onions. Add chicken broth; set aside.

3. Rinse the thawed turkey under cold water and pat dry with paper towels. Using your fingers, carefully loosen the skin around the entire bird. Chop the butter mixture into small pieces. Place half of the butter pieces under the skin of the turkey. Rub the remaining butter pieces on the outside of the skin. Season inside and outside of the turkey with salt and pepper. Stuff turkey cavity with remaining onions, fresh herbs, and lemon slices. (Truss if desired.) Insert a pop-up thermometer at an angle (about 3 inches down from the neck cavity and 2 inches from the breast bone).

4. Place turkey, breast side up, on a rack over the vegetables in the roasting pan. Place in preheated oven and reduce temperature to 325 degrees F.

5. Roast for 1 hour. Then, basting with pan juices every 20 minutes, continue roasting about 3 hours more or until thermometer pops up or an instant-read thermometer inserted into the inside thigh muscle registers 180 degrees F.

Turkey with Dumplings

Prep 20 minutes   **Cook** 20 minutes
Makes 6 servings

MEAL 2

2	tablespoons butter
2	stalks celery, chopped
1	package (8-ounce) sliced fresh mushrooms
1	cup frozen chopped onions, *Ore-Ida®*
1	teaspoon crushed garlic, *Gourmet Garden®*
3	cups leftover turkey, chopped
2	cups frozen peas and carrots, *Birds Eye®*
1	can (49-ounce) reduced-sodium chicken both, *Swanson®*
2	packets (0.87 ounces each) turkey gravy mix, *McCormick®*
1½	cups baking mix, *Bisquick®*
¾	cup sour cream
2	tablespoons fresh sage, finely chopped
1	teaspoon coarse-grind black pepper, *McCormick®*

1. In a Dutch oven, melt butter over medium heat. Add celery, mushrooms, onions, and garlic; cook for 2 minutes. Add turkey and peas and carrots. Add broth. Whisk in turkey gravy mix. Bring to a boil over medium heat. Meanwhile, for dumpling dough, in a medium bowl, combine baking mix, sour cream, sage, and pepper, stirring until a soft dough forms. When soup comes to a boil, drop heaping tablespoons of the dumpling dough into soup. Maintain a low boil and cook, uncovered, for 10 minutes. Cover and cook for 10 minutes more. Dumplings are done when they are dry in the center. Ladle soup and dumplings into warm soup bowls and serve hot.

Open-Face Turkey Mornay

Prep 25 minutes   **Bake** 20 minutes
Makes 4 servings

MEAL 3

1	can (14-ounce) reduced-sodium chicken broth, *Swanson®*
2	tablespoons butter
1	package (1.6-ounce) Alfredo sauce mix, *Knorr®*
1¾	cups finely shredded Swiss cheese
2½	cups sliced leftover turkey
4	English muffins, split, *Thomas®*
4	slices Canadian-style bacon
1	tomato, sliced
1	can (15-ounce) asparagus spears, drained and rinsed, *Green Giant®*

1. Preheat oven to 350 degrees F. Line a baking sheet with foil. For Mornay sauce, in a saucepan, combine broth and butter over medium heat; whisk in Alfredo sauce mix. Bring to a boil, stirring constantly. Reduce heat; simmer for 2 minutes. Add 1¼ cups of the Swiss cheese, stirring just until melted. Remove from heat. Divide sliced turkey among split English muffins. Top with Canadian bacon, tomato, and asparagus; place on a baking sheet. Spoon the Mornay sauce over; top with the remaining ½ cup Swiss cheese. Bake in preheated oven about 20 minutes or until heated through and cheese is bubbling and just starting to brown.

Down-Home Pot Roast

Prep 20 minutes   **Bake** 3 hours
Stand 5 minutes   **Marinate** 4 hours
Makes 12 servings

Who's to know these spicy enchiladas and Yankee dips were once pot roast, served with potatoes and carrots? Wrap the extra meat in a tortilla with chiles and cheeses, then reinvent it on a roll with mashed potatoes and onion jus.

6	pounds beef chuck roast
2	cups red wine
1	cup olive oil and vinegar salad dressing, *Newman's Own*®
2	tablespoons Worcestershire sauce, *Lea & Perrins*®
1	envelope (0.6-ounce) zesty Italian salad dressing mix, *Good Seasons*®
2	tablespoons canola oil
2	brown or yellow onions, sliced
3	stalks celery, cut into 2-inch pieces
4	cups lower-sodium beef broth, *Swanson*®
2	packets (1.5 ounces each) meat loaf seasoning mix, *McCormick*®
3	pounds baby Yukon gold or fingerling potatoes, cut in half
1	pound baby carrots
	Celery leaves (optional)

1. Place meat in a large zip-top plastic bag. In a medium bowl, whisk together wine, olive oil and vinegar salad dressing, Worcestershire sauce, and dry Italian salad dressing mix. Pour over meat in bag. Seal bag; turn to coat meat. Marinate in refrigerator for 4 hours to overnight, turning bag occasionally.

2. Preheat oven to 325 degrees F. Remove meat from marinade and pat dry with paper towels. Discard marinade. In a large skillet, heat oil over medium heat. Add meat and brown on all sides. Place in roasting pan and set aside.

3. Add onion and celery to same skillet; cook for 3 minutes. Stir in broth and meat loaf seasoning; bring to a boil. Remove from heat and carefully pour over meat. Cover tightly with aluminum foil. Bake for 2 hours.

4. Remove roast from oven and add potatoes and carrots. Re-cover pan. Bake for 1 hour more. Remove roast, potatoes, and carrots from pan. Let meat stand for 5 minutes before slicing. Strain pan juices and set aside. Slice meat against the grain. Serve meat with potatoes, carrots, and strained pan juices. Garnish with celery leaves (optional).

Beefy Enchiladas

Prep 25 minutes **Bake** 40 minutes
Makes 6 servings

MEAL 2

2	cans (15 ounces each) red enchilada sauce, *Las Palmas*®
2½	cups leftover beef pot roast, shredded
2	cups shredded Mexican blend cheese, *Sargento*®
½	cup frozen chopped onions, *Ore-Ida*®
½	cup sliced black olives, *Early California*®
½	cup canned diced green chiles, *Ortega*®
12	corn tortillas
	Canola oil
	Chopped lettuce and tomato

1. Preheat oven to 350 degrees F. Evenly coat the bottom of a 9×13-inch baking dish with ½ cup of the enchilada sauce; set aside. Place beef, cheese, onions, olives, and green chiles in separate small bowls; set aside. Pour 1½ cups of the remaining enchilada sauce into a pie plate; set aside. To soften tortillas, in a small skillet, heat a small amount of canola oil over medium heat. Add tortillas, one at a time; fry for 5 seconds per side. Drain tortillas on paper towels.

2. To assemble enchiladas, dip a softened tortilla into sauce in pie plate. Put some of the beef, onions, olives, and green chiles across center of the tortilla; sprinkle with some of the cheese. Roll up tightly; place, seam side down, in prepared baking dish. Repeat to make 12 enchiladas. Spread any sauce remaining in the pie plate over enchiladas; top with remaining cheese. Cover loosely with foil. Bake in preheated oven for 40 to 45 minutes. Place the remaining enchilada sauce in a microwave-safe bowl; microwave on high setting (100 percent power) about 2 minutes or until hot. Serve sauce over hot enchiladas. Top with lettuce and tomato.

Yankee "Dip" Sandwiches

Start to Finish 25 minutes
Makes 4 sandwiches

MEAL 3

2	cups leftover potatoes
¼	cup ranch salad dressing, *Hidden Valley*®
2	tablespoons butter
2	cups leftover beef jus
1	envelope (1.1-ounce) beefy onion soup mix, *Lipton*®
2	cups leftover beef pot roast, sliced
4	French rolls, split

1. Place potatoes in a microwave-safe bowl. Cover and microwave on high setting (100 percent power) for 3 to 4 minutes or until hot. Add ranch dressing and butter; mash. Cover; set aside.

2. In a large skillet, stir together beef jus and dry onion soup mix. Bring to a simmer over medium heat. Add sliced roast and heat through.

3. Spread bottom half of each roll with mashed potatoes. Using tongs, remove beef from jus; divide among sandwiches. Quickly dip top half of each roll in jus; place on top of sandwiches. Serve immediately with ramekins of extra jus on the side.

Caribbean Pork Shoulder

Prep 20 minutes **Roast** 3 hours
Stand 5 minutes **Makes** 10 servings

Caribbean one night, Italian the next, Mexican a third. It all comes from one pork shoulder, simmered with tropical fruit. Shred it with sausage and mozzarella marinara, then bake with ziti for pasta-perfect leftovers. It's thrice as nice spooned into a taco shell.

6	pounds pork shoulder roast
2	teaspoons salt
2	teaspoons cinnamon, *McCormick*®
1	teaspoon ground black pepper, *McCormick*®
1	cup all-purpose flour
3	tablespoons canola oil
2	sweet onions, sliced
1	can (14-ounce) reduced-sodium chicken broth, *Swanson*®
1	can (11.5-ounce) mango nectar, *Kern's*®
¼	cup packed brown sugar, *C&H*®
4	teaspoons Jamaican jerk seasoning, *McCormick*®
2	red, orange, and/or green bell peppers, seeded and cut into strips
1	bag (12-ounce) frozen mango chunks, thawed, *Dole*®
	Fresh mango slices (optional)
	Fresh cilantro sprigs (optional)

1. Preheat oven to 325 degrees F. Cut meat into three or four pieces. Season meat with salt, cinnamon, and pepper. Dredge in flour. In a large skillet, heat oil over medium-high heat. Add meat and brown on all sides, working in batches if necessary. Place meat in a roasting pan and set aside.

2. Add onions to the skillet; cook for 3 minutes. Add broth, nectar, brown sugar, and jerk seasoning; bring to a boil. Carefully pour broth mixture over meat. Cover tightly with aluminum foil. Roast for 2 hours.

3. Remove from oven and add red peppers and mangoes. Re-cover pan and roast for 1 hour more.

4. Remove meat, mangoes, and vegetables from pan. Let meat stand for 5 minutes before slicing. Strain pan juices and set aside. Slice meat against the grain. Serve hot with mangoes, vegetables, and strained pan juices. Garnish with mango slices and cilantro sprigs (optional).

Baked Ziti with Spicy Pork

Prep 20 minutes **Cook** 10 minutes
Bake 20 minutes **Makes** 8 servings

MEAL 2

	Olive oil cooking spray, *Pam®*
16	ounces cut ziti pasta, *Barilla®*
2	tablespoons extra virgin olive oil, *Bertolli®*
1	package (3-ounce) sliced pancetta
1	pound spicy Italian sausage, casings removed
3	cups leftover pork roast, cut into bite-size pieces
1	jar (26-ounce) marinara sauce, *Newman's Own®*
1	can (15-ounce) tomato sauce, *Hunt's®*
1	can (14-ounce) reduced-sodium beef broth, *Swanson®*
2	cups shredded mozzarella cheese, *Sargento®*
¼	cup grated Parmesan cheese, *DiGiorno®*

1. Preheat oven to 400 degrees F. Spray a 9×13-inch baking pan with cooking spray; set aside. In a large pot of boiling salted water, cook pasta about 10 minutes or until just barely tender. Drain pasta; set aside.

2. In a large straight-sided skillet, heat oil over medium-high heat. Add pancetta; fry until crispy. Using a slotted spoon, transfer pancetta to paper towels to drain. Add sausage to skillet; cook until browned, using a wooden spoon to break up into small pieces. Add pork, marinara sauce, tomato sauce, and beef broth; stir until combined. Bring to a boil. Remove from heat; stir in cooked ziti. Transfer pork mixture to prepared baking dish; sprinkle with mozzarella and Parmesan. Bake in preheated oven for 20 minutes. Serve hot.

Carnitas Tacos

Start to Finish 20 minutes
Makes 6 servings

MEAL 3

2	cans (15 ounces each) pinto beans, *Bush's®*
1	can (10-ounce) Mexican-style diced tomatoes, *Rotel®*, drained
1	teaspoon Mexican seasoning, *McCormick®*
3	cups leftover pork roast, shredded
¾	cup jus from pork roast, chicken broth, or water
1	package (1.25-ounce) reduced-sodium taco seasoning, *McCormick®*
12	small 6-inch flour tortillas, warmed
	Shredded lettuce, chopped bell pepper, cilantro sprigs, and/or chopped onions (optional)

1. Combine pinto beans, tomatoes, and Mexican seasoning in a medium saucepan. Simmer over medium heat for 7 to 8 minutes. Meanwhile, combine pork, jus, and taco packet in a large skillet. Bring to a boil. Reduce to simmer for 5 minutes.

2. Make tacos by topping each tortilla with a spoonful of beans and some pork. Serve with lettuce, pepper, cilantro, and/or onion (optional).

Spicy Molasses-Glazed Ham

Prep 20 minutes **Roast** 2½ hours
Makes 20 servings

One family-size ham makes a succulent entrée, then encores as fun-to-eat skewers and a down-home casserole. A molasses glaze pairs with pineapple to make luau-like kabobs, then takes on a pepper Jack kick in a cheesy meat and potato hot dish.

7	to 8 pounds cooked ham
20	whole cloves, *McCormick®*
½	cup molasses, *Grandma's®*
¼	cup packed dark brown sugar, *C&H®*
¼	cup ginger preserves, *Robertson's®*
¼	cup dark rum, *Myers's®*
1	fresh habañero chile, stem and seeds removed, finely chopped (see tip, page 77)
1	tablespoon minced ginger, *Gourmet Garden®*
½	teaspoon dry mustard, *Coleman's®*
	Pineapple tops (optional)
	Whole habañero chiles (optional)

1. Preheat oven to 325 degrees F. Line a roasting pan with aluminum foil; set aside.

2. Cut the thick layer of fat and skin from ham and discard. Score the ham in a diamond pattern by making shallow diagonal cuts at 1-inch intervals; insert whole cloves in centers of diamonds. Place ham in roasting pan. Roast in preheated oven for 1 hour.

3. Meanwhile, for glaze, in a medium saucepan, combine molasses, brown sugar, ginger preserves, rum, chile, ginger, and dry mustard. Bring to a boil; reduce heat. Simmer, uncovered, stirring constantly until sugar and preserves are dissolved. Remove from heat.

4. After ham has roasted for 1 hour, baste with glaze and continue roasting about 1½ hours more or until an instant-read thermometer inserted in ham (away from bone) registers 130 to 140 degrees F, basting ham with glaze every 15 minutes. Garnish with pineapple tops and habañero chiles (optional).

Southern Ham Casserole

MEAL 2

Olive oil cooking spray, *Pam®*
2 tablespoons butter
1 package (8-ounce) fresh sliced mushrooms
2 cups leftover ham
1 cup frozen chopped onions, *Ore-Ida®*
1 cup shredded pepper Jack cheese, *Tillamook®*
1 can (10.75-ounce) condensed cream of mushroom soup, *Campbell's®*
½ cup sour cream
1¼ pounds red potatoes, thinly sliced

1. Preheat oven to 350 degrees F. Spray a 2½-quart casserole dish with cooking spray; set aside. In a large skillet, melt butter over medium-high heat. Add mushrooms; cook about 5 minutes or until golden and liquid has evaporated. Add ham and onions; heat through. In a large bowl, stir together cheese, soup, and sour cream. Add ham mixture and potatoes. Toss to coat. Place in prepared casserole dish. Cover and bake in preheated oven for 1 hour. Serve hot.

South Seas Kabobs

MEAL 3

1½ pounds leftover ham, cut into 1-inch pieces
1 pound pineapple spears, cut into 1-inch pieces, *Ready Pac®*
1 sweet onion, cut into 1-inch pieces
2 red, orange, and/or yellow bell peppers, cut into 1-inch pieces
1 jar (9-ounce) plum sauce, *Lee Kum Kee®*
¼ cup pineapple juice, *Dole®*
2 tablespoons chili sauce, *Heinz®*
2 teaspoons Jamaican jerk seasoning, *McCormick®*

1. Preheat broiler. Line a baking sheet with foil. Alternately thread ham, pineapple, and vegetables on 4 long skewers.* Set aside on prepared baking sheet. In a medium saucepan, stir together plum sauce, pineapple juice, chili sauce, and jerk seasoning. Simmer over medium heat for 5 minutes.

2. Brush kabobs with plum sauce mixture. Broil in preheated broiler 6 to 8 inches from heat for 8 to 12 minutes or until starting to brown and vegetables are crisp-tender, turning kabobs to brown evenly. Serve hot kabobs with any remaining plum sauce mixture.

*NOTE: If using bamboo skewers, soak them in water for at least 1 hour.

Provence-Style Leg of Lamb with Gravy

Prep 20 minutes   **Roast** 2 hours 20 minutes
Stand 30 minutes   **Marinate** 4 hours
Makes 10 servings

French herbs and wine make leg of lamb a traditional dinner. Carve and serve, then add the leftovers to a hearty cassoulet with sausage and beans. It's a different dish the third time around, in a gingery Asian hot pot with stir-fry veggies, noodles, and bok choy.

MEAL 1

1	6-pound boneless leg of lamb
2	cups red wine
1	cup cranberry juice cocktail, *Ocean Spray®*
2	tablespoons extra virgin olive oil, *Bertolli®*
1	tablespoon crushed garlic, *Gourmet Garden®*
1	tablespoon dried rosemary, crushed, *McCormick®*
1	tablespoon herbes de Provence, *McCormick®*
1	teaspoon coarsely ground black pepper
2	tablespoons flour
	Assorted roasted vegetables (optional)

1. Place leg of lamb in large zip-top plastic bag. Set aside. In a medium bowl, whisk together 1 cup of the red wine, cranberry juice, oil, garlic, rosemary, herbes, and pepper. Pour over lamb. Seal bag; turn to coat lamb. Marinate in refrigerator for 4 hours to overnight.

2. Preheat oven to 450 degrees F. Remove lamb from marinade and place in roasting pan. Discard marinade. Let lamb stand for 30 minutes to come to room temperature.

3. Roast lamb in preheated oven for 20 minutes. Reduce oven to 325 degrees F. Continue roasting for 2 to 2 ½ hours or until an instant-read thermometer inserted in meat (away from bone) is 160 degrees F for medium. Transfer to carving board and let stand while preparing pan sauce.

4. For pan sauce, drain juices and fat from roasting pan. Skim off fat, reserving 2 tablespoons. Place roasting pan over medium heat and add reserved fat. Whisk in flour, scraping up browned bits; cook for 2 minutes. Add enough water to the reserved pan juices to equal 1 cup liquid. Add liquid and the remaining 1 cup wine to roasting pan. Cook and stir until simmering; cook for 1 minute more.

5. Carve lamb. Serve hot with assorted roasted vegetables (optional) and pan sauce.

Bordeaux Beans with Lamb

Prep 20 minutes **Bake** 1 ¼ hours
Makes 8 servings

MEAL 2

2	tablespoons extra virgin olive oil, *Bertolli*®
1	cup frozen chopped onions, *Ore-Ida*®
1	teaspoon crushed garlic, *Gourmet Garden*®
1	can (14.5-ounce) petite diced tomatoes, *S&W*®
1	cup Bordeaux wine
⅓	cup real bacon crumbles, *Hormel*®
1	teaspoon herbes de Provence, *McCormick*®
½	teaspoon freshly ground black pepper
3	cans (15 ounces each) white beans, drained and liquid reserved, *S&W*®
3	cups leftover lamb roast, cut into bite-size pieces
1	cup seasoned bread crumbs, *Progresso*®
3	tablespoons butter, melted

1. Preheat oven to 350 degrees F. In a large skillet, heat oil over medium-high heat. Add onions and garlic; cook for 2 to 3 minutes or until onions are tender. Add tomatoes; cook for 1 minute. Add wine, bacon crumbles, herbes, and pepper; cook for 5 minutes. Remove from heat.

2. Spread one-third of the beans in the bottom of a 2½- to 3-quart casserole dish. Top with half of the lamb and half of the tomato mixture. Repeat layering, ending with beans. Add enough of the reserved bean liquid to come just to the top the beans. In a small bowl, stir together bread crumbs and butter; sprinkle over top of casserole. Bake in preheated oven for 1¼ hours. Every 20 minutes or so, push bread crumbs down so liquid bubbles up and forms a crust.

Lamb Firepot with Vegetables

Start to Finish 25 minutes
Makes 8 servings

MEAL 3

2½	quarts reduced-sodium chicken broth, *Swanson*®
¼	cup dry sherry, *Christian Brothers*®
1	tablespoon minced ginger, *Gourmet Garden*®
2	teaspoons crushed garlic, *Gourmet Garden*®
1	bag (14-ounce) stir-fry vegetables, *C&W*®
1	pound bok choy, chopped
1	cup broken vermicelli noodles, *Barilla*®
1½	pounds leftover lamb, cut into strips (about 3 cups)
1	box (12-ounce) firm tofu, cut into ½-inch cubes, *Mori-Nu*®
¼	cup sliced scallions (green onions)

1. In a large pot, bring broth, sherry, ginger, and garlic to a boil. In a microwave-safe bowl, microwave stir-fry vegetables on high setting (100 percent power) for 5 minutes.

2. Add bok choy and vermicelli to hot broth mixture; cook for 5 minutes. After vermicelli has cooked for 5 minutes, add stir-fry vegetables, lamb, and tofu. Bring to a simmer; simmer for 2 minutes. Remove from heat; stir in scallions. Serve hot.

Lavish Leftovers

1. **Hash it out.** Use leftover vegetables and meats as fillings for old-fashioned omelets, scrambles, and hash. Almost any flavor combo works well with eggs.

2. **Think outside the wok.** Just about any leftover meat or seafood can be sliced and stir-fried with precut vegetables to make a complete meal. Just add some purchased stir-fry sauce and serve with packaged cooked rice.

3. **Make comfort food quick.** Heat frozen and/or precut veggies, precooked potatoes, and leftover meat or chicken with equal parts of jarred gravy and broth to make a hearty stew. Serve with crusty bread for dipping.

4. **Date your leftovers.** Place leftovers in shallow containers and label with the date and dish name. Discard leftovers after four days in the refrigerator or a month in the freezer. When in doubt, throw it out.

5. **Bag a salad.** Spruce up last night's leftover meat as a healthy lunch. Brown-bag the extras with packaged greens, veggies, and dressing.

The Recipes

Polenta Shepherd's Pie

Prep 20 minutes   **Bake** 30 minutes
Makes 6 servings

   Nonstick cooking spray, *Pam®*
4 slices bacon
1 onion, chopped
3 cups chopped leftover chicken, turkey, pork, or beef
2 cups frozen mixed vegetables, *Birds Eye®*
1 can (14-ounce) vegetable, chicken, or beef broth, *Swanson®*
1 packet (1.6-ounce) garlic and herb sauce mix, *Knorr®*
1 tube (24-ounce) precooked polenta, *San Gennaro®*
½ stick (¼ cup) butter, melted

1. Preheat oven to 350 degrees F. Lightly spray a 2-quart baking dish with cooking spray; set aside.

2. In a large skillet, fry bacon over medium heat until browned but not crispy. Remove bacon with a slotted spoon and drain all but 2 tablespoons of the fat from the skillet. Add onion; cook for 2 minutes more. Add leftover chicken to the skillet; cook for 2 minutes more. Stir in vegetables, broth, and sauce mix. Bring to a boil; reduce heat. Simmer, uncovered, for 1 minute. Transfer to prepared baking dish and set aside.

3. Finely crumble polenta into a medium bowl; stir in butter. Sprinkle polenta mixture over chicken mixture. Place baking dish on baking sheet. Bake in preheated oven for 30 minutes.

Easy Cacciatore

Prep 15 minutes   **Cook** 10 minutes
Makes 6 servings

3 cups leftover chicken, turkey, or pork cut into bite-size pieces
1 can (28-ounce) diced tomatoes with garlic, oregano, and basil, *Del Monte®*
1 bag (16-ounce) frozen yellow and green zucchini, *C&W®*
1 cup reduced-sodium chicken broth, *Swanson®*
½ cup white wine
2 tablespoons tomato paste, *Hunt's®*
2 teaspoons Italian seasoning, *McCormick®*
1 teaspoon crushed garlic, *Gourmet Garden®*
   Salt and black pepper
   Hot cooked pasta

1. In a large pot or Dutch oven, combine leftover chicken, undrained tomatoes, zucchini, broth, wine, tomato paste, Italian seasoning, and garlic. Bring to a boil over medium heat; reduce heat. Simmer, uncovered, for 10 minutes. Season to taste with salt and pepper. Serve with hot cooked pasta.

Fabulous Frittata

Prep 10 minutes   **Bake** 35 minutes
Stand 5 minutes   **Makes** 6 servings

This Italian egg pie is easier than an omelet, especially when you use a shredded cheese blend. Eggs go well with almost any meat or vegetable, so use your imagination—and your leftovers—to make a creative anytime meal.

	Butter-flavor cooking spray, *Pam*®
1	**cup precooked potatoes with herbs and garlic,** *Reeser's*®
1	**cup chopped leftover ham, pork, turkey, or shrimp**
1	**cup shredded Colby and Jack cheese blend,** *Sargento*®
4	**eggs**
1½	**cups milk**
1	**teaspoon salt-free all-purpose seasoning,** *McCormick*®
½	**teaspoon salt**
¼	**teaspoon black pepper**

1. Preheat oven to 400 degrees F. Spray 9-inch glass pie plate with butter-flavor cooking spray.

2. Add potatoes, leftover ham, and cheese to prepared pie plate. Set aside. In a medium bowl, whisk together eggs, milk, salt-free seasoning, salt, and pepper. Pour into pie plate. Bake in preheated oven for 35 to 45 minutes or until eggs are set in center. Let cool on a wire rack for 5 minutes before serving.

Ravioli with Parma Rosa Sauce

Start to Finish 40 minutes
Makes 4 servings

The pink sauce looks so lovely, you would hardly guess it's a combo of jarred ingredients. The delicate contradiction of tart tomatoes and buttery cheeses is a match for almost any meat.

FOR RAVIOLI:
1½	cups leftover chicken, turkey, pork, or beef cut into small chunks
½	cup frozen chopped onions, *Ore-Ida*®
¼	cup chopped fresh parsley
2	tablespoons grated Parmesan cheese, *DiGiorno*®
2	teaspoons crushed garlic, *Gourmet Garden*®
3	eggs
1	teaspoon water
48	wonton wrappers, *Dynasty*®

FOR PARMA ROSA SAUCE:
1	jar (16-ounce) Alfredo sauce, *Classico*®
1	can (8-ounce) tomato sauce, *Hunt's*®
¼	cup grated Parmesan cheese, *DiGiorno*®
1	teaspoon Italian seasoning, *McCormick*®
	Fresh snipped chives (optional)

1. To make Ravioli, in a food processor fitted with a metal blade, combine leftover chicken, onions, parsley, Parmesan cheese, and garlic. Pulse several times until mixture is finely chopped. Transfer to a medium bowl. Lightly beat 2 of the eggs and stir into meat mixture. Set aside.

2. In a small bowl, lightly whisk together the remaining egg and the water; set aside. Place a spoonful of the chicken mixture in the center of a wonton wrapper. Brush edges of wrapper with egg mixture and cover with another wonton wrapper. Press edges together, making sure edges are completely sealed.* Cover with a clean kitchen towel so that ravioli does not dry out. Repeat with remaining chicken mixture and wonton wrappers to make 24 ravioli total.

3. For Parma Rosa Sauce, in a medium saucepan, combine Alfredo sauce, tomato sauce, Parmesan cheese, and Italian seasoning. Bring to a boil; reduce heat. Simmer, uncovered, for 5 minutes. Cover and keep warm.

4. In a pot of boiling salted water, cook ravioli for 6 to 8 minutes or until tender. Top ravioli with Parma Rosa Sauce. Garnish with chives (optional).

*NOTE: If desired, cut the edges of the ravioli with a fluted pastry wheel.

Individual Wellingtons

Prep 30 minutes   **Cook** 10 minutes
Chill 15 minutes   **Bake** 25 minutes
Makes 4 servings

My sister Kim and I fell in love with beef Wellington in Paris, and I was determined to make its extravagance accessible. I swap cognac for Madeira and a creamy Boursin® cheese for foie gras and truffles. The rich puff pastry and jus make it a clever way to stretch portions.

2	tablespoons butter
1	cup chopped fresh mushrooms
1	cup frozen chopped onions, *Ore-Ida®*
2	teaspoons crushed garlic, *Gourmet Garden®*
½	teaspoon salt
2	tablespoons cognac
1	sheet (from 17-ounce box) frozen puff pastry, thawed, *Pepperidge Farms®*
1	box (5.2-ounce) semisoft pepper cheese, softened, *Boursin®*
2	cups coarsely chopped leftover chicken, turkey, pork, beef, or lamb
1	egg, lightly beaten
1	teaspoon water

1. In a large skillet, melt butter over medium heat. Add mushrooms, onions, garlic, and salt. Cook about 10 minutes or until juices released from mushrooms have evaporated. Add cognac; cook until cognac has evaporated.

2. On a lightly floured surface, roll out puff pastry to a 12-inch square. Cut into four 6-inch squares. Divide cheese among puff pastry squares, placing cheese in center of each square. Top with leftover chicken; top with mushroom mixture.

3. In a small bowl, lightly whisk together egg and the water. Brush the edges of the puff pastry squares with the egg mixture. Pull the corners of each pastry square to the center; pinch edges closed. Place, seam sides down, on a baking sheet. Chill in refrigerator for 15 minutes.

4. Preheat oven to 400 degrees F. Remove Wellingtons from refrigerator and brush tops of pastries with the remaining egg mixture. Bake in preheated oven about 25 minutes or until puffed and golden brown.

Empanadas

Prep 25 minutes   **Bake** 18 minutes
Makes 8 servings

FOR EMPANADAS:
Nonstick cooking spray, *Pam*®
2   cups finely chopped leftover chicken, turkey, pork, or beef
1   jar (16-ounce) chunky salsa, *Newman's Own*®
2   cups shredded Mexican-blend cheese, *Sargento*®
1   egg, lightly beaten
1   teaspoon water
2   cans (16.3 ounces each) refrigerated biscuits, *Pillsbury*®

FOR RANCHERO SAUCE:
2   cans (10 ounces each) diced tomatoes with chiles
          (original or mild), *Rotel*®
1   cup frozen chopped onions, *Ore-Ida*®
½   cup roasted red bell peppers, diced, *Delallo*®
2   teaspoons ground cumin, *McCormick*®
        Salt and black pepper

1. Preheat oven to 375 degrees F. Lightly spray 2 baking sheets with cooking spray; set aside.

2. For Empanadas, in a large bowl, stir together leftover chicken, salsa, and cheese. Set aside. In a small bowl, lightly whisk together egg and the water. Set aside. Remove biscuits from cans. On a lightly floured surface, roll each biscuit to a circle 6 inches in diameter.

3. Place ¼ cup of the chicken-salsa mixture off center on a rolled-out biscuit. Brush the edges of the biscuit with some of the egg mixture. Fold biscuit in half; use the tines of a fork to crimp the edges. Place on prepared baking sheet. Repeat with the remaining biscuits and the remaining chicken-salsa mixture. Brush egg mixture over empanadas. Bake for 18 to 20 minutes or until golden brown.

4. Meanwhile, for Ranchero Sauce, in a food processor, combine tomatoes, onions, red peppers, and cumin; pulse until smooth. Transfer to a medium saucepan; simmer over medium heat until ready to serve. Season to taste with salt and pepper. Serve hot empanadas with Ranchero Sauce.

Chilaquiles

Prep 25 minutes   **Bake** 10 minutes
Makes 6 servings

Unlike nachos, which are served crispy, chilaquiles are made by baking the tortilla chips and turkey strips in salsa with a topping of melted cheese. It's a good way to use stale chips—the flavors mingle, so you'll never know!

2	tablespoons canola oil
1½	cups chopped red onion
3	cups shredded leftover cooked turkey, chicken, or beef
1	can (10-ounce) diced tomatoes and green chiles, *Rotel*®
1	can (4-ounce) diced green chiles, *Ortega*®
1	jar (16-ounce) chunky salsa, *Newman's Own*®
	Salt and black pepper
5	cups tortilla chips
1½	cups shredded Mexican-blend cheese, *Sargento*®
¼	cup chopped fresh cilantro

1. Preheat oven to 400 degrees F. In a large oven-going skillet, heat oil over medium-high heat. Add onion; cook until soft. Add leftover turkey, undrained diced tomatoes, and undrained chiles; cook and stir about 2 minutes or until heated through. Stir in salsa and heat for 2 minutes more. Season to taste with salt and pepper. Stir in tortilla chips. Top with cheese.

2. Bake in preheated oven for 10 to 15 minutes or until cheese melts. Remove from oven and sprinkle with cilantro.

Farmhouse Hash

Prep 20 minutes   **Bake** 1 hour
Broil 4 minutes   **Makes** 6 servings

½	pound smoked bacon, chopped
1	bag (20-ounce) frozen roasted potatoes, *Ore-Ida®*
2	cups finely chopped leftover beef, chicken, pork, turkey, or lamb
1	cup frozen chopped onions, finely chopped, *Ore-Ida®*
1	cup reduced-sodium beef or reduced-sodium chicken broth, *Swanson®*
½	cup roasted red bell peppers, chopped, *Delallo®*
½	cup frozen chopped green bell peppers, *Pictsweet®*
1	teaspoon crushed garlic, *Gourmet Garden®*
	Salt and black pepper

1. Preheat oven to 350 degrees F. In a large skillet, cook bacon just until crispy; remove bacon with slotted spoon. Use 1 to 2 tablespoons of the bacon fat to grease a 9×13-inch baking pan; set aside.

2. In a large bowl, combine potatoes, leftover beef, onions, broth, red peppers, green peppers, and garlic. Season to taste with salt and black pepper. Cover and bake in preheated oven for 1 hour. Remove from oven.

3. Preheat broiler. Broil 6 to 8 inches from heat for 4 to 5 minutes or until crisp.

Chinese Casserole

Prep 20 minutes   **Bake** 30 minutes
Makes 4 servings

	Nonstick cooking spray, *Pam*®
1	**can (10.75-ounce) condensed cream of chicken and mushroom soup, *Campbell's*®**
⅓	**cup dry sherry, *Christian Brothers*®**
2	**tablespoons stir-fry seasoning mix, *Kikkoman*®**
2	**cups leftover chicken, pork, turkey, or shrimp cut into bite-size pieces**
1	**can (8-ounce) sliced water chestnuts, *La Choy*®**
½	**cup cashews, *Planters*®**
4	**stalks celery, finely chopped**
2	**scallions (green onions), sliced diagonally**
1	**can (5-ounce) chow mein noodles, *La Choy*®**
	Scallions (green onions), sliced lengthwise (optional)

1. Preheat oven to 350 degrees F. Spray a 1½-quart casserole dish with cooking spray and set aside.

2. In a small bowl, whisk together chicken and mushroom soup, sherry, and stir-fry seasoning until smooth.

3. In a large bowl, combine leftover chicken, water chestnuts, cashews, celery, and scallions. Stir in three-quarters of the chow mein noodles. Stir in soup mixture.

4. Transfer to prepared casserole dish. Top with the remaining chow mein noodles. Bake in preheated oven for 30 to 35 minutes. Garnish with scallions (optional).

Singapore Noodles

Start to Finish 30 minutes
Makes 4 servings

2	tablespoons canola oil
4	slices bacon, finely chopped
1	can (6-ounce) tiny shrimp
1	cup chopped yellow onion
1	tablespoon minced ginger, *Gourmet Garden*®
2	teaspoons crushed garlic, *Gourmet Garden*®
4	cups water
2	packages (3 ounces each) chicken-flavor ramen noodles, *Top Ramen*®
2	teaspoons red curry powder, *McCormick*®
1½	cups finely shredded leftover chicken, turkey, or pork
4	scallions (green onions), finely chopped
¼	cup dry sherry, *Christian Brothers*®
	Fresh chives (optional)

1. In a large skillet or wok, heat oil over medium-high heat. Add bacon, shrimp, onion, ginger, and garlic. Cook for 2 minutes. Reduce heat to medium-low; cook for 15 minutes, stirring occasionally.

2. Meanwhile, in a large saucepan, bring the water to a boil; add ramen noodles and cook for 3 minutes. Drain and set aside.

3. Add curry powder and seasoning packets from ramen noodles to bacon mixture; stir to combine. Turn heat to high and add leftover chicken and noodles. Using a pair of large forks, toss to combine. Add scallions and sherry and toss until sherry is absorbed. Garnish with chives (optional).

Vietnamese Noodle Salad

Start to Finish 20 minutes
Makes 4 servings

2	boxes (5.6 ounces each) sesame stir-fry rice noodles, *Thai Kitchen*®
6	cups boiling water
¼	cup rice vinegar, *Marukan*®
½	cup canola oil
2	cups spring lettuce mix, *Fresh Express*®
2	cups bean sprouts
2	cups seeded, chopped cucumber
1½	cups shredded leftover chicken, beef, pork, or shrimp
½	cup chopped fresh mint leaves
⅓	cup chopped fresh basil leaves

1. Remove noodles from noodle kits and place in a large bowl. Pour the boiling water over noodles; soak for 3 to 5 minutes or until softened and tender. Drain and rinse under cold water. Set aside.

2. Meanwhile, for dressing, in a medium bowl, combine vinegar and seasoning packets from noodle kits. Slowly whisk in canola oil. Whisk in sesame oil from noodle kits. Set aside.

3. Arrange lettuce, sprouts, cucumber, chicken, and noodles on 4 chilled plates. Sprinkle with mint and basil. Serve with dressing.

Sweet Solutions

1. Make a disposable pastry bag. Fill a zip-top bag with frosting, seal the top, and snip off a bottom corner for piping. If you need to change tips, use a coupler and pastry tips in the bag.

2. Change the flavor. Use a fruit juice in place of water in mixes. White cranberry or white grape juice adds sweetness to a white cake without changing the color.

3. Bakery from a box. Make any oil-based cake mix taste fresh from the bakery by substituting the amount of oil called for with the same amount of melted butter.

4. Fresh flavors. To make canned frosting taste divine, beat it in a mixing bowl with ½ teaspoon vanilla, peppermint, or coconut extract, or any other flavoring.

5. Make fruit fancy. Melt chocolate chips in the microwave until smooth. Dip strawberries or sliced bananas and oranges in the chocolate and place on a waxed paper-lined sheet pan. Serve the fruit as dessert or use it to decorate cakes, pies, and other treats.

The Recipes

Chocolate-Cherry Dump Cake

Prep 10 minutes **Bake** 50 minutes
Makes 12 servings

1	box (18.25-ounce) devil's food cake mix, *Betty Crocker*®
1½	cans (21 ounces each) cherry pie filling, *Comstock*® *More Fruit* or *Wilderness*® *More Fruit*
1	can (15-ounce) pitted tart pie cherries, drained, *Oregon*®
1½	cups chopped walnuts, *Planters*®
1	stick (½ cup) butter, cut into slices
	Vanilla bean ice cream (optional)

1. Prepare cake mix according to package directions. Pour cherry pie filling and drained tart pie cherries into an ungreased 9×13-inch baking pan. Using a rubber spatula, stir cherry mixture; spread evenly in baking pan. Spread prepared cake mix over top. Sprinkle with walnuts. Dot with sliced butter.

2. Bake in preheated oven for 50 to 55 minutes or until cake layer is cooked through and fruit is bubbling. Serve warm with ice cream (optional).

Peach Melba Refrigerated Cake

Prep 20 minutes **Chill** 4 hours
Makes 12 servings

4	cups vanilla wafer cookies, *Nilla*®
5	tablespoons butter, melted
1	can (15-ounce) peach slices, drained, *S&W*®
1½	cups milk
1	box (5.1-ounce) instant vanilla pudding and pie filling, *Jell-O*®
1	teaspoon raspberry extract, *McCormick*®
1	cup frozen whipped dessert topping, thawed, *Cool Whip*®
1	can (21-ounce) raspberry pie filling, *Comstock*® *More Fruit* or *Wilderness*® *More Fruit*

1. In a food processor, process vanilla wafer cookies to make fine crumbs. Add butter; pulse until mixture comes together. Press crumb mixture into bottom of a 9×9-inch square baking pan. Arrange peach slices on top of crumb mixture; set aside.

2. In a large bowl, whisk together milk, pudding mix, and raspberry extract for 2 minutes; let stand about 3 minutes or until thick. Stir in whipped topping. Spoon mixture over peaches; using a rubber spatula, smooth the top. Chill in refrigerator for at least 4 hours before serving. Spoon raspberry pie filling evenly over top.

Mini Baked Alaskas

Prep 20 minutes   **Bake** 4 minutes
Makes 6 servings

Call it the five-minute finale. It looks every bit as impressive as the famed dinner party dessert, and the exquisite intermingling of hot and cold is just as shiver-inducing. Klondike® bars let you skip a step, so all you have to do is make the meringue and brown it under the broiler.

1	cup plus 4 teaspoons liquid egg whites (at room temperature), *All Whites*®
½	teaspoon cream of tartar, *McCormick*®
⅛	teaspoon salt
¾	cup sugar
1	teaspoon vanilla extract, *McCormick*®
6	½-inch-thick slices purchased pound cake
6	(4.5 ounces each) ice cream bars, *Klondike*®

1. Preheat the oven to 400 degrees F. Line a baking sheet with foil; set aside. Chill 6 dessert plates.

2. For meringue, in a medium bowl, combine egg whites, cream of tartar, and salt; beat with an electric mixer on high speed until soft peaks form. Gradually add sugar, beating constantly until stiff peaks form. Add the vanilla; mix well.

3. Trim each pound cake slice to same size as an ice cream bar. Place pound cake slices on prepared baking sheet. Unwrap ice cream bars; set one bar on each pound cake slice to make six sandwiches. Spread meringue evenly over each sandwich, sealing completely; make small decorative peaks on top.

4. Bake in preheated oven about 4 minutes or until lightly browned. Transfer each baked Alaska to a chilled dessert plate. Serve immediately.

Margarita Pie

Prep 15 minutes   **Bake** 10 minutes
Makes 8 servings

When my best friend, Colleen, and I get together, this tops the menu. Frozen margarita mix and a ready-made crust make it quick to fix. Chill it in the freezer to firm it up, then rim it with lime wheels—just like a real 'rita.

4	egg yolks
1	can (14-ounce) sweetened condensed milk, *Eagle Brand*®
½	cup frozen margarita mixer, thawed, *Bacardi*®
¼	cup orange tequila, *Jose Cuervo*®
2	or 3 drops green food coloring, *McCormick*®
1	(9-inch) shortbread crumb crust, *Keebler*® *Ready Crust*®
	Frozen whipped topping, thawed, *Cool Whip*®
	Chopped, toasted macadamia nuts (optional)
	Lime slices (optional)

1. Preheat oven to 350 degrees F. In a large bowl, beat yolks with an electric mixer on medium speed about 2 minutes or until pale. Add sweetened condensed milk; beat about 4 minutes or until light and fluffy. Using a rubber spatula, scrape down side of bowl. Add margarita mixer, tequila, and green food coloring; beat until well mixed. Pour mixture into shortbread crumb crust.

2. Bake in preheated oven for 10 to 15 minutes or just until set. Cool in pan on a wire rack. Chill in refrigerator until ready to serve. Use a pastry bag fitted with a star tip (or a heavy-duty zip-top bag with a corner snipped off) to pipe whipped topping around the edge of the pie. Sprinkle with chopped macadamia nuts and garnish with lime slices (optional).

STRAWBERRY MARGARITA PIE: Prepare as directed, except subsitute frozen strawberry margarita mixer for the margarita mixer, red food coloring for the green food coloring, and strawberry slices for the lime slices.

Banana-Peach-Mango Crumble

Prep 10 minutes   **Bake** 45 minutes
Makes 8 servings

	Nonstick vegetable cooking spray, *Pam*®
2	bananas, cut into 1-inch-thick slices
1	bag (16-ounce) frozen mango chunks, thawed, *Dole*®
1	can (15-ounce) peach slices, drained and ¼ cup juice reserved, *S&W*®
¼	cup packed brown sugar, *C&H*®
¼	cup mango-flavor rum, *Malibu*®
2	tablespoons quick-cooking tapioca, *Minute*®
10	mini crumb donuts

1. Preheat oven to 350 degrees F. Spray an 8-inch square baking pan or 8 small ramekins with cooking spray and set aside.

2. In a large bowl, combine bananas, mango chunks, and peaches with the reserved juice, brown sugar, rum, and tapioca. Stir mixture and spoon into prepared baking pan. Crumble donuts over top of fruit mixture.

3. Bake in preheated oven for 45 to 55 minutes or until fruit is tender and edges are bubbly. Serve warm.

Apple Pie Parfaits

Start to Finish 10 minutes
Makes 4 servings

1	can (20-ounce) apple pie filling, *Comstock® More Fruit* or *Wilderness® More Fruit*
⅓	cup candied walnuts, chopped, *Emerald®*
¼	teaspoon allspice, *McCormick®*
16	oatmeal cookies, *Mother's Cookies®*
½	cup butterscotch caramel sauce, *Mrs. Richardson's®*
1	pint vanilla ice cream, *Häagen-Dazs®*
	Candied walnuts, *Emerald®*

1. In a medium bowl, stir together apple pie filling, the ⅓ cup chopped candied walnuts, and the allspice. Set aside.

2. Crumble two oatmeal cookies into the bottom of each of four parfait glasses. Top each with 1 tablespoon caramel sauce. Divide half of the apple mixture among the four glasses. Add a scoop of ice cream to each glass. Repeat layering, ending with ice cream. Sprinkle each parfait with candied walnuts.

Blueberry Ricotta Crepe Cups

Prep 20 minutes **Bake** 9 minutes
Cool 5 minutes **Makes** 6 servings

	Nonstick vegetable cooking spray, *Pam®*
¼	cup ricotta cheese, *Precious®*
¼	cup sour cream
1	egg
2	tablespoons sugar
1	cup blueberry pie filling, *Comstock® More Fruit* or *Wilderness® More Fruit*
1	tablespoon all-purpose flour
6	purchased crepes, *Freida's®*

1. Preheat oven to 325 degrees F. Spray twelve 2½-inch muffin cups with cooking spray and set aside.

2. In a medium bowl, whisk together ricotta cheese, sour cream, egg, and sugar until smooth. Stir in ¼ cup of the blueberry pie filling and the flour until well mixed; set aside. Using a sharp knife, cut each crepe in half. Fold each half over to make a square. Fit each crepe square into one of the prepared muffin cups to make 12 crepe cups. Fill each crepe cup with 1 tablespoon of the ricotta mixture.

3. Bake in preheated oven for 9 to 10 minutes or until ricotta mixture is set. Cool for 5 minutes in muffin cups on wire rack.

4. Carefully remove crepe cups from muffin cups. Top each crepe cup with 1 tablespoon of the remaining blueberry pie filling.

Pretzel Fudge

Prep 20 minutes   **Cook** 10 minutes
Cool 3 hours   **Makes** 24 pieces

Nonstick vegetable cooking spray, *Pam*®
2   **cups plus 24 individual tiny pretzels,** *Rold Gold*®
4   **cups sugar**
1   **can (12-ounce) evaporated milk,** *Carnation*®
1   **stick (½ cup) butter**
1   **bag (12-ounce) semisweet chocolate chips,** *Nestlé*®
30   **large marshmallows,** *Jet-Puffed*®
¾   **cup honey-roasted peanuts,** *Planters*®

1. Spray a 9×13-inch baking pan with cooking spray; set aside.

2. Place 2 cups of the pretzels in a large zip-top bag. Press out air and seal bag. Using a rolling pin, roll over pretzels until crushed; set aside.

3. In a large saucepan, combine sugar, evaporated milk, and butter; bring to a boil over medium heat. Cook, uncovered, for 10 minutes, stirring constantly with a wooden spoon.

4. Remove from heat. Add chocolate chips and marshmallows; stir until smooth. Add crushed pretzels and peanuts, stirring until well mixed.

5. Pour into prepared baking pan. Place the remaining 24 tiny pretzels on top of fudge (four across and six down), spacing evenly. Lightly press tiny pretzels into fudge. Cool at room temperature about 3 hours or until set. Cut into pieces.

Tropical Brittle

Prep 15 minutes   **Bake** 10 minutes
Microwave 11 ½ minutes
Makes 1 pound

¾	cup sweetened shredded coconut, *Baker's*®
2	tablespoons butter
1	cup packed dark brown sugar, *C&H*®
½	cup mango syrup, *Margie's*®
2	tablespoons light-color corn syrup, *Karo*®
1	cup chopped macadamia nuts, *Mauna Loa*®
1	teaspoon baking soda

1. Preheat oven to 350 degrees F. Pour coconut onto a baking sheet. Toast coconut in preheated oven about 10 minutes or until golden brown, stirring occasionally. Remove and cool to room temperature.

2. Line another baking sheet with parchment paper, leaving a ½-inch overhang on one side. Grease paper with 1 tablespoon of the butter; set aside.

3. In a large microwave-safe bowl, stir together brown sugar, mango syrup, and corn syrup. Microwave on high setting (100 percent power) for 7 minutes.* Carefully remove bowl from microwave; stir in macadamia nuts. Microwave on high setting (100 percent power) for 4½ minutes. Using baking mitts, remove bowl from microwave; stir in toasted coconut and the remaining 1 tablespoon butter. Use caution as bowl will be extremely hot. Quickly stir in baking soda (mixture will rise). Immediately pour onto prepared baking sheet; quickly spread, using the back of a spoon. Cool completely.

4. Pull parchment paper from baking sheet to remove. Break brittle into pieces.

*NOTE: This brittle was made using an 800-watt microwave. If you are using a microwave with different wattage, adjust the time accordingly.

NOTE: To store, place brittle in an airtight container. Store for up to 1 week at room temperature.

Magic Bars

Prep 15 minutes   **Bake** 35 minutes
Makes 12 servings

5	cups chocolate graham sticks, *Honey Maid*®
¾	cup plus 2 tablespoons butter, melted
1½	cups chopped pecans, *Diamond*®
¾	cup butterscotch chips, *Nestlé*®
½	cup white baking chips, *Nestlé*®
2	cups sweetened shredded coconut, *Baker's*®
1	can (14-ounce) sweetened condensed milk, *Eagle Brand*®

1. Preheat oven to 325 degrees F. In a food processor, process chocolate graham sticks to make fine crumbs. Add melted butter. Cover and pulse until mixture comes together. Press crumb mixture into the bottom of an ungreased 9×13-inch baking pan.

2. Sprinkle pecans over chocolate graham crust. Sprinkle evenly with butterscotch chips and white baking chips. Sprinkle coconut over top. Pour sweetened condensed milk evenly over entire mixture.

3. Bake in preheated oven for 35 to 40 minutes or until set in center. Cool in pan on a wire rack. Cut into bars.

Brownie Truffles

Prep 20 minutes   **Chill** 1 hour
Makes 28 (1-tablespoon) truffles

Forget the mixing and melting—just add water to a package of fudge brownie mix, scoop into balls, and chill.

1   box (21.3-ounce) dark chocolate brownie mix (with chocolate syrup pouch), *Betty Crocker*®
¼   cup water
2   tablespoons light-color corn syrup, *Karo*®
     Coatings, such as sweet flaked coconut, nonpareils, nut topping, and/ or colored sprinkles

1. In a large bowl, stir together dry brownie mix, chocolate syrup from pouch, the water, and corn syrup until well mixed.

2. Pour each desired coating into separate pie plates. Scoop up 1 tablespoon of the brownie mixture; using slightly wet hands, shape mixture into a smooth ball. Roll ball into desired coating to cover entire ball. Place on ungreased baking sheet. Repeat to make 28 truffles, rinsing hands when mixture becomes too sticky to roll. Chill in refrigerator for 1 hour. Serve chilled or at room temperature.

NOTE: To store the truffles, layer between waxed paper in an airtight container. Store for 3 to 4 days at room temperature, 1 week in the refrigerator, or up to 3 months in the freezer.

Pantry Bark

Prep 10 minutes   **Microwave:** 5 minutes
Cool 4 hours   **Makes** 2 pounds 3 ounces candy

Five straight-from-the-pantry ingredients and you have an energy-rich treat. Honey Oat Chex® cereal, pretzels, and peanut butter make it crunchy.

      Nonstick vegetable spray coating, *Pam*®
22   chocolate wafer cookies, *Nabisco*® *Famous*
1½   cups honey nut bite-size square cereal, crushed, *Chex*®
⅓   cup peanut butter chips, *Reese's*®
5   cups milk chocolate chips, *Nestlé*®
1   cup white fudge-covered pretzels, *Flipz*®

1. Spray a 9×13-inch baking pan with cooking spray. In a food processor, process chocolate wafer cookies to make fine crumbs. Pour crumbs evenly into bottom of prepared baking pan. Sprinkle cereal and peanut butter chips over top; set aside.

2. Place chocolate chips in a large microwave-safe bowl. Microwave on medium setting (50 percent power) about 5 minutes or until melted, stirring every 1½ minutes. Pour melted chocolate over top of the mixture in baking pan; spread with rubber spatula. Top with pretzels. Cool at room temperature about 4 hours or until firm. Cut into pieces.

NOTE: To store, place in an airtight container. Store at room temperature for up to 1 week.

Quick-Fix Holiday

1. Expect unexpected guests. Shortbread, biscotti, pirouettes, truffles, and fine chocolates go well with coffee or liqueur and can be kept indefinitely.

2. Give a frozen pie scratch appeal. Brush the top of a frozen apple pie with melted butter and sprinkle with cinnamon sugar during the last ten minutes of baking. When serving, sprinkle the plate with cinnamon and serve warm with a spoonful of mascarpone cheese lightly dusted with cinnamon.

3. Add aromatics. Heat purchased gravy with bay leaves, peppercorns, dried herbs, or pearl onions to make it smell homemade. Pour it in a gravy boat and it'll be your little secret.

4. Greet guests with no-bake sweets. Dip candy canes in melted chocolate and let them harden on waxed paper. Arrange on a tray for guests or wrap in bow-tied cellophane to give as gifts.

5. Show your holiday spirits. Skewer fresh cranberries on a 4-inch bamboo skewer for a colorful cocktail swizzle. Or drop a few berries into a glass of Champagne to add a splash of color.

The Recipes

173

Sausage-Stuffed Mushrooms

Prep 25 minutes **Bake** 15 minutes
Makes 28 servings

	Nonstick cooking spray, *Pam*®
28	large white button mushrooms (each about 2 inches in diameter)
1	tablespoon extra virgin olive oil, *Bertolli*®
1	pound spicy pork sausage, *Jimmy Dean*®
2	teaspoons Greek seasoning, *McCormick*®
½	teaspoon salt
1	package (10-ounce) frozen chopped spinach, cooked and well drained, *Birds Eye*®
1	jar (4-ounce) chopped pimiento, drained, *Dromedary*®
⅓	cup shredded Romano cheese, *DiGiorno*®
2	eggs, lightly beaten

1. Preheat oven to 350 degrees F. Lightly spray a baking sheet with cooking spray. Wipe mushrooms clean but do not get them wet. Remove mushroom stems; reserve. Lightly spray mushroom caps inside and out with cooking spray; set aside. Finely chop the mushroom stems; set aside.

2. In a large skillet, heat oil over medium-high heat. Break up sausage into skillet; add chopped mushroom stems, Greek seasoning, and salt. Cook until sausage is crumbled and cooked through. Transfer sausage mixture to a bowl. Add spinach, pimiento, Romano cheese, and eggs; stir to combine.

3. Stuff each mushroom with about 2 tablespoons of the sausage mixture, pressing firmly into the mushroom. Place stuffed mushrooms on prepared baking sheet. Bake in preheated oven for 15 to 20 minutes just until mushrooms are tender and stuffing is heated through. Sprinkle with additional Romano cheese (optional).

Gorgonzola-Pear Toasts

Start to Finish 25 minutes
Makes 40 pieces

1	baguette, cut into ¼-inch-thick slices
2	tablespoons extra virgin olive oil, *Bertolli*®
1	package (8 ounces) cream cheese, *Philadelphia*®
4	ounces crumbled Gorgonzola cheese, *Athenos*®
2	cans (15 ounces each) sliced pears in juice, drained, *Del Monte*®
½	cup candied pecans, chopped, *Emerald*®
2	tablespoons finely chopped fresh parsley

1. Preheat oven to 400 degrees F. Lightly brush 1 side of each baguette slice with oil. Place baguette slices on baking sheet. Toast in preheated oven for 5 to 7 minutes or just until beginning to brown. Let cool.

2. Meanwhile, in a small bowl, combine cream cheese and Gorgonzola cheese, stirring until well mixed. Spread toasts with cheese mixture. Top with pear slices and chopped candied pecans. Sprinkle with parsley.

Pork Tenderloin with Holiday Chutney

Prep 25 minutes **Roast** 10 minutes
Stand 10 minutes **Makes** 8 servings

My Grandma Lorraine loved chutney because you can make it ahead of time using dried fruits from the cupboard. Just treat the tenderloins to an oil and spice rub and pull the chutney out of the fridge. The pumpkin pie spices smell heavenly—and save time too.

FOR HOLIDAY CHUTNEY:

¾	cup dried apricots, chopped, *Sun-Maid*®
¾	cup white cranberry juice, *Ocean Spray*®
½	cup frozen chopped onions, *Ore-Ida*®
¾	cup red wine vinegar
2	tablespoons sugar
2	teaspoons pumpkin pie spice, *McCormick*®
¾	cup dried cranberries, *Ocean Spray*®
¼	cup chopped pecans, *Diamond*®

FOR PORK TENDERLOIN:

1	tablespoon dried sage, *McCormick*®
1	tablespoon garlic salt, *Lawry's*®
2	teaspoons black pepper
1	2½-pound pork tenderloin, trimmed
2	tablespoons extra virgin olive oil, *Bertolli*®
	Hot rice (optional)

1. For Holiday Chutney, in a medium saucepan, combine apricots, white cranberry juice, and onions. Bring to a boil; reduce heat. Simmer, uncovered, for 5 minutes. Transfer apricot mixture to a medium bowl; set aside. Add vinegar, sugar, and pumpkin spice to the saucepan. Simmer until sugar has dissolved. Stir in cranberries; let stand for 5 minutes. Strain apricot mixture; stir into cranberry mixture. Stir in pecans. Set aside.

2. For Pork Tenderloin, preheat oven to 400 degrees F. In a small bowl, stir together sage, garlic salt, and pepper. Using your fingers, rub sage mixture on all sides of pork tenderloin. Set aside.

3. In a large skillet, heat oil over medium-high heat. Cook pork in hot oil until browned on all sides. Transfer to a baking sheet. Roast pork in preheated oven for 10 to 15 minutes or until an instant-read thermometer inserted in center of tenderloin registers 160 degrees F.

4. Let tenderloin stand for 5 minutes before slicing. Place tenderloin slices on a bed of hot rice (optional). Serve with Holiday Chutney.

Orange- and Bourbon-Grilled Turkey Tenderloins

Prep 15 minutes   **Marinate** 4 to 6 hours
Stand 20 minutes   **Grill** 4 minutes per side
Makes 6 servings

2	pounds turkey breast tenderloins
½	cup orange juice, *Minute Maid®*
¼	cup bourbon, *Jim Beam®*
2	tablespoons molasses, *Grandma's®*
1	tablespoon Dijon mustard, *Grey Poupon®*
1	tablespoon soy sauce, *Kikkoman®*
2	teaspoons pumpkin pie spice, *McCormick®*
2	tablespoons canola oil
1	teaspoon salt
1	teaspoon freshly ground black pepper

1. Rinse turkey with cold water and pat dry with paper towels. Place turkey in a large zip-top plastic bag; set aside. In a small bowl, whisk together orange juice, bourbon, molasses, mustard, soy sauce, and pumpkin pie spice; pour over turkey in bag. Squeeze air from bag and seal. Marinate in refrigerator for at least 4 hours or up to 6 hours. Remove turkey from marinade; discard marinade. Let stand at room temperature for 20 minutes.

2. Set up grill for direct grilling over medium-high heat. Oil grate when ready to start cooking. Pat tenderloins dry with paper towels. Brush with the 2 tablespoons oil; season with salt and pepper. Place turkey on hot oiled grill. Cook for 4 to 6 minutes per side or until cooked through and no longer pink in the center (170 degrees F). Slice tenderloins.

Mandarin-Cranberry Rice Dressing

Start to Finish 20 minutes
Makes 4 servings

1	box (6.2-ounce) fast-cooking long grain and wild rice, *Uncle Ben's®*
1	cup frozen seasoning-blend vegetables, *Pictsweet®*
¾	cup reduced-sodium chicken broth, *Swanson®*
1	can (11-ounce) mandarin orange segments, drained, *Geisha®*
½	cup whole berry cranberry sauce, *Ocean Spray®*
⅓	cup chopped pecans, *Diamond®*

1. In a medium saucepan, combine rice, vegetable blend, and chicken broth. Bring to a boil; reduce heat. Cover and simmer for 5 minutes. Remove from heat and let stand about 5 minutes or until broth is absorbed. Stir in mandarin oranges, cranberry sauce, and pecans.

Glazed Roast Duck

Prep 30 minutes   **Roast** 1 hour 40 minutes
Stand 5 minutes   **Makes** 4 servings

FOR ROAST DUCK:
1   4- to 5-pound duck
1   tablespoon kosher salt
1   teaspoon black pepper
1   teaspoon poultry seasoning, *McCormick®*
½   teaspoon ground cumin, *McCormick®*
1   recipe Mandarin-Cranberry Rice Dressing, cooled (see recipe, page 178)

FOR ORANGE-HONEY GLAZE:
1   cup orange marmalade, *Smucker's®*
½   cup honey, *Sue Bee®*
2   tablespoons *Grand Marnier®*
    Garnishes, such as fresh sage leaves, roasted garlic bulbs, and/or orange slices (optional)

1. For Roast Duck, preheat oven to 475 degrees F. Remove neck and giblets from duck cavity. Discard or save for another purpose. Rinse duck with cold water, inside and out. Pat dry with paper towels. Using a long-tined fork, lightly prick duck skin several times to help fat render out.

2. In a small bowl, combine salt, pepper, poultry seasoning, and cumin; sprinkle over duck inside and out.

3. Stuff duck with prepared Mandarin-Cranberry Rice Dressing. Use wooden toothpicks to close and secure skin around cavity opening. Place stuffed duck in a roasting pan, breast side up. (Ducks contain a lot of fat and do not require basting.) If duck comes with pop-up thermometer, insert it at an angle (about 2 inches down from the neck cavity and 1 inch from the breast bone).

4. Place duck in preheated oven; lower oven temperature to 375 degrees F. Roast about 1 hour 40 minutes to 2 hours 5 minutes or until pop-up thermometer pops or until an instant-read thermometer inserted in inside muscle of thigh registers 165 degrees F.

5. Meanwhile, for Orange-Honey Glaze, in a medium bowl, stir together orange marmalade, honey, and Grand Marnier®. About 10 to 15 minutes before duck is done, pour glaze over duck. Remove duck from oven; tent with aluminum foil. Let stand for 5 to 10 minutes before carving. Garnish with sage, garlic, and/or orange slices (optional).

Red Currant Lamb Chops

Prep 15 minutes   **Roast** 30 minutes
Stand 10 minutes   **Makes** 4 servings

½   cup red currant jelly, *Knott's*®
3   tablespoons soy sauce, *Kikkoman*®
2   tablespoons Dijon mustard, *Grey Poupon*®
2   racks of lamb (about 1½ pounds each)
2   teaspoons garlic salt, *Lawry's*®
1   teaspoon black pepper
    Watercress (optional)

1. Preheat oven to 400 degrees F. In a saucepan, for red currant glaze, combine jelly, soy sauce, and mustard. Cook over medium heat until jelly has melted, stirring frequently. Remove from heat.

2. Season lamb on all sides with garlic salt and pepper. Place lamb, bone sides down, on a wire rack in a roasting pan. Roast in preheated oven for 30 to 35 minutes for medium doneness (160 degrees F). (After the first 10 minutes of roasting, baste lamb every 10 minutes with currant glaze.)

3. Remove from oven. Tent with aluminum foil; let stand for 10 minutes. Cut lamb into individual chops. Meanwhile, bring any remaining red currant glaze to a boil. Brush chops with remaining glaze. Garnish with watercress (optional).

Golden Margarita Cranberry Molds

Prep 15 minutes   **Chill** 5½ hours
Makes 12 servings

2¼   cups cranberry juice cocktail, *Ocean Spray*®
1   box (0.6-ounce) sugar-free cranberry gelatin, *Jell-O*®
¾   cup ready-to-drink golden margarita, *Jose Cuervo*®
1   can (16-ounce) whole berry cranberry sauce, *Ocean Spray*®
½   cup chopped pecans, *Diamond*®
2   tablespoons grated orange zest
    Orange curls (optional)
    Chopped toasted pecans (optional)

1. In a medium saucepan, bring the cranberry juice to a boil. Transfer to a medium bowl; add gelatin, stirring until gelatin is completely dissolved. Stir in margarita. Refrigerate for 1½ to 2 hours or until mixture begins to set.

2. Stir in cranberry sauce, pecans, and orange zest. Divide mixture evenly among desired cocktail glasses. Refrigerate at least 4 hours or up to 24 hours to set. Garnish with orange curls and toasted pecans (optional).

Turkey Drumstick Gravy

Prep 25 minutes   **Cook** 1 hour
Makes 5 cups

2	whole turkey drumsticks, cooked
6	cups cold water
1	large onion, quartered
¾	stick (6 tablespoons) butter
½	cup quick-mixing flour, *Wondra®*
	Salt and black pepper
	Chopped crisp-cooked bacon (optional)

1. In a large saucepan, combine drumsticks, cold water, and quartered onion. Bring to a boil over medium-high heat; reduce heat. Simmer, uncovered, for 1 hour. Pour stock through fine-mesh strainer; discard drumsticks and onion. In a medium saucepan, melt butter over medium heat. When butter has melted, whisk in flour to form a roux. Cook roux for 1 minute, stirring constantly. Slowly whisk in turkey stock. Bring to a boil; reduce heat. Simmer, uncovered, about 5 minutes or until gravy has thickened. Season to taste with salt and pepper. Pour into gravy boat or bowl. Garnish with crisp-cooked bacon (optional).

Pink Peppercorn Gravy

Start to Finish 10 minutes
Makes 2½ cups

2¼	cups reduced-sodium chicken broth, *Swanson®*
¼	cup cognac
1	packet (1.6-ounce) garlic and herb sauce mix, *Knorr®*
1	packet (0.87-ounce) turkey or brown gravy mix, *McCormick®*
2	tablespoons butter
2	teaspoons pink peppercorns, crushed, *The Spice Hunter®*
	Crushed pink peppercorns and fresh thyme sprigs (optional)

1. In a medium saucepan, whisk together chicken broth, cognac, dry sauce mix, and dry gravy mix; stir in butter and peppercorns. Bring to a boil over medium heat, stirring constantly. Reduce heat. Simmer, uncovered, about 3 minutes or until thickened. Garnish with pink peppercorns and fresh thyme sprigs (optional).

Lemon-Chive Gravy

Start to Finish 10 minutes
Makes 2 cups

1	jar (12-ounce) turkey, chicken, brown, or mushroom gravy, *Heinz®*
2	tablespoons butter
2	tablespoons lemon juice, *Minute Maid®*
1	tablespoon finely chopped fresh chives
1	tablespoon dry sherry, *Christian Brothers®*
	Salt and black pepper
	Fresh chives (optional)

1. In a medium saucepan, combine gravy, butter, lemon juice, chives, and sherry. Cook over medium heat just until simmering. Season to taste with salt and pepper. Garnish with fresh chives (optional).

Corn Bread Pudding

Prep 10 minutes **Bake** 1 hour
Makes 12 servings

Store-bought corn bread isn't as moist as my Grandma Dicie's, but turn it into a country-style custard with creamed corn and cheese and you'll get all the credit without all the work. Water chestnuts add an unexpected crunch.

	Nonstick cooking spray, *Pam*®
1	egg
1	cup reduced-sodium chicken broth, *Swanson*®
1	pound purchased corn bread, cut into 1-inch cubes
1	can (14.75-ounce) cream-style corn, *Green Giant*®
1	cup canned french-fried onions, *French's*®
1	cup shredded Monterey Jack cheese (4 ounces), *Sargento*®
1	can (8-ounce) sliced water chestnuts, *La Choy*®
2	tablespoons Italian herb marinade mix, *Durkee*® *Grill Creations*®

1. Preheat oven to 350 degrees F. Spray a 2½-quart casserole dish with cooking spray. Set aside.

2. In a small bowl, beat together egg and chicken broth.

3. In a large bowl, combine corn bread, corn, onions, cheese, water chestnuts, and marinade mix. Pour egg mixture over corn bread mixture; stir to combine. Transfer to the prepared casserole dish. Bake in preheated oven for 1 hour.

Apricot Bread Stuffing

Prep 20 minutes **Bake** 30 minutes
Makes 12 servings

1	pound maple sausage, *Jimmy Dean*®
1¼	cups frozen seasoning blend vegetables *Pictsweet*®
1	box (12-ounce) seasoned dressing mix, *Mrs. Cubbison's*®
1	stick (½ cup) butter
½	cup chopped pecans, *Diamond*®
1	cup dried apricots, chopped, *Sun Maid*®
1½	cups reduced-sodium chicken broth, *Swanson*®
	Fresh rosemary sprigs (optional)

1. Preheat oven to 350 degrees F. Lightly grease a 3-quart casserole dish; set aside.

2. In a large skillet, combine sausage and vegetable blend; cook over medium heat until sausage is browned. Transfer to a large bowl. Add dressing mix, the ½ cup butter, the pecans, and dried apricots; stir to combine. Slowly stir in broth.

3. Transfer dressing mixture to prepared casserole dish. Cover and bake in preheated oven for 30 minutes. Garnish with fresh rosemary (optional).

Buttered Brussels Sprouts and Carrots

Prep 5 minutes
Makes 10 servings

1	bag (16-ounce) frozen Brussels sprouts, *Birds Eye*®
2	cups frozen sliced carrots, *Birds Eye*®
1	cup frozen chopped onions, *Ore-Ida*®
1	tablespoon water
¾	stick (6 tablespoons) butter
⅓	cup chopped walnuts
1	teaspoon lemon juice, *Minute Maid*®

1. In a large microwave-safe bowl, combine Brussels sprouts, carrots, onions, and the water. Cover and microwave on high setting (100 percent power) for 3 to 5 minutes or until Brussels sprouts are hot throughout, stirring once or twice. Drain well. Stir in butter. Cover and microwave 2 to 3 minutes more or until butter is melted, stirring once or twice. Add walnuts and lemon juice; toss until well mixed.

Early Peas and Haricots Verts in Garlic Herb Sauce

Prep 15 minutes
Makes 12 servings

1	bag (16-ounce) frozen haricots verts (green beans), *C&W*®
1	bag (16-ounce) frozen early harvest peas, *C&W*®
1	tablespoon water
4	strips bacon, chopped
1	cup slivered red onions
1¼	cups half-and-half or light cream
¼	cup cognac
1	packet (1.6-ounce) garlic herb sauce mix, *Knorr*®
	Salt and black pepper

1. In a microwave-safe bowl, combine frozen green beans and peas. Add the water; cover and heat on high setting (100 percent power) for 8 to 10 minutes or just until vegetables are tender, stirring once.

2. Meanwhile, in a large saucepan, brown chopped bacon. Drain all but 1 tablespoon of the bacon fat from the pan. Add slivered onions; cook until softened. Add half-and-half and cognac to saucepan; whisk in dry garlic herb sauce mix. Bring to a boil, stirring constantly; reduce heat. Simmer, uncovered, until thickened.

3. Drain green beans and peas. Add to pan with sauce; stir to coat vegetables. Season to taste with salt and pepper.

Bourbon Sweet Potato Pie

Prep 30 minutes   **Bake** 1 hour 8 minutes
Cool 2 hours   **Makes** 8 servings

1	frozen deep-dish piecrust, *Marie Callender's*®
1	bag (24-ounce) frozen cut sweet potatoes, *Ore-Ida® Steam n' Mash*
¼	cup butter, melted
1¼	cups sugar
2	eggs, lightly beaten
1	can (5-ounce) evaporated milk, *Carnation*®
¼	cup bourbon, *Jim Beam*®
2	teaspoons pumpkin pie spice, *McCormick*®
	Purchased caramel sauce (optional)
	Chopped toasted pecans (optional)

1. Preheat oven to 400 degrees F. Let piecrust thaw for 10 minutes. Prick the bottom and sides of crust with a fork. Bake on a baking sheet in preheated oven for 8 minutes.

2. Meanwhile, prepare sweet potatoes as directed on package. Mash cooked sweet potatoes with butter. Stir in sugar, eggs, evaporated milk, bourbon, and pumpkin spice; pour into pie shell. Leaving pie on baking sheet, bake for 10 minutes.

3. Reduce oven to 350 degrees F and continue baking for 50 to 60 minutes or until a knife inserted 1 inch off-center comes away clean. Cool for 2 hours before slicing. Drizzle individual slices with caramel sauce and sprinkle with toasted pecans (optional).

Dark Chocolate Coffee

Start to Finish 5 minutes
Makes 1 serving

1   shot chocolate liqueur, *Godiva®*
1   shot coffee liqueur, *Kahlua®*
½   shot dark crème de cacao
       Strong black coffee
       Whipped cream
       Cocoa powder, *Hershey's®*
       Chocolate shavings (optional)

1. In an Irish coffee mug, combine chocolate liqueur, coffee liqueur, and crème de cacao. Fill mug with coffee. Top with whipped cream and dust with cocoa powder. Garnish with chocolate shavings (optional).

Pomegranate Champagne Punch

Start to Finish 10 minutes
Makes 16 servings

3   cups pomegranate juice, *Pom®*
3   cups white cranberry juice, *Ocean Spray®*
½   cup pomegranate liqueur, *Pama®*
2   bottles (750 milliliters each) extra-dry Champagne, *Korbel®*
       Ice

1. In a punch bowl, combine pomegranate juice, white cranberry juice, and pomegranate liqueur. Slowly add the Champagne; stir. Serve in ice-filled glasses.

White Chocolate Eggnog

Start to Finish 10 minutes
Makes 6 servings

4   cups eggnog
1   cup white baking morsels, *Nestlé®*
1   teaspoon vanilla extract, *McCormick®*
¼   teaspoon rum extract, *McCormick®*
       Whipped topping, *Cool Whip®*
       Ground nutmeg, *McCormick®*
       Grated white baking bar (optional)

1. In a medium saucepan, combine 1 cup of the eggnog and the white baking morsels. Cook over medium heat, stirring constantly, until morsels have completely melted. Stir in the remaining 3 cups eggnog, the vanilla extract, and rum extract. Cook until heated through, stirring occasionally. Pour into mugs. Top each serving with a spoonful of whipped topping and a dash of nutmeg. Garnish with white baking bar shavings (optional)

NOTE: For an adult version, add a shot of spiced rum (*Captain Morgan®*) and/or a shot of white chocolate liqueur (*Godiva®*) to each serving.

Party Pairings

1. Be creative with containers. Packaged candies, chocolate-covered nuts, and snack mix look special served in footed glass bowls, vases, and containers scattered around the party area.

2. Serve it bite-size. Pizza, sandwiches, and artisan bread go further—and look more party-friendly—sliced into nibbles. One or two bites per serving is ideal.

3. Use your slow cooker. Mulled wine, hot toddies, and party favorites such as meatballs and fondue are a snap to serve out of slow cookers.

4. Create a party cupboard. Stash entertaining essentials such as plates, glasses, flatware, candles, napkins, and table fabrics. White dishes go with everything and showcase food to perfection.

5. Keep cocktails self-serve. Keep it simple by serving red and white wine, sparkling water, and one party punch. Serve drinks in glass pitchers with trays of glasses. Keep extra pitchers in the refrigerator to swap out the empties.

The Recipes

Party Pizza Squares

Prep 15 minutes   **Bake** 10 minutes
Makes 20 pizza squares

½	pound bulk Italian sausage
2	Italian bread shells (8-inch), *Boboli*®
1	jar (14-ounce) pizza sauce, *Ragu*®
1	cup chopped red and/or green bell pepper
½	cup sliced ripe olives
1	cup shredded Italian cheese blend, *Sargento*®
¼	cup coarsely chopped fresh basil

1. Preheat oven to 400 degrees F. In a large skillet, brown sausage over medium heat, breaking up large clumps with a wooden spoon. Drain any fat; set aside.

2. Place bread shells on a large sheet pan. Divide pizza sauce between shells, spreading to edges. Divide the cooked sausage crumbles, chopped peppers, olives, and shredded cheese blend between the shells, sprinkling each evenly over each shell.

3. Bake in preheated oven for 10 to 15 minutes or until cheese is melted and bubbly. Remove from oven. Sprinkle chopped basil over pizza. Cut each pizza into about 10 squares. Place on a platter; serve hot.

NOTE: For an even easier appetizer, bake a frozen pizza according to package directions. Remove from oven; sprinkle with ¼ cup chopped basil. Cut into squares; serve on platter.

Champagne Cheers

Start to Finish 5 minutes
Makes 2 servings

2	tablespoons cherry brandy, *Kirschwasser*®
	Extra-dry Champagne, *Korbel*®
2	maraschino cherries, *Mezzetta*®

1. Set out cocktail glasses. Add 1 tablespoon cherry brandy to each glass. Slowly pour in Champagne. Drop a cherry into each glass. Serve immediately.

Asiago-Ham Pinwheels

Prep 20 minutes   **Bake** 15 minutes
Makes 16 pinwheels

1	sheet puff pastry, thawed, *Pepperidge Farm®*
2	tablespoons apricot preserves, *Smucker's®*
1½	tablespoons Dijon mustard, *Grey Poupon®*
¼	cup currants, *Sun-Maid®*
¼	cup shredded Asiago cheese, *DiGiorno®*
6	ounces deli ham, thinly sliced
	Water

1. Preheat oven to 400 degrees F. Line 2 baking sheets with parchment paper and set aside. Unroll puff pastry sheet on a lightly floured surface; use a rolling pin to roll into 14×11-inch rectangle.

2. In a small bowl, stir together preserves and mustard; spread over puff pastry. Sprinkle with currants; sprinkle cheese on top of currants. Arrange ham slices on top of cheese. Starting with a short side, roll rectangle up into a spiral, rolling tightly. Using a pastry brush, brush edge with water; press seam to seal. Using a sharp knife, cut pastry roll into ½-inch-wide slices. Arrange pinwheels on baking sheets.

3. Bake for 15 to 18 minutes or until puffed and golden brown. Transfer pinwheels to a wire rack; let cool for 5 minutes. Serve warm.

Star-Tini

Start to Finish 15 minutes
Makes 2 servings

	Ice
4	shots vodka, *Smirnoff®*
2	shots *Cointreau®*
2	shots white cranberry juice, *Ocean Spray®*
2	lime wedges
	Orange slices and/or star fruit (carambola) slices (optional)

1. Fill a cocktail shaker with ice. Pour vodka, Cointreau®, and cranberry juice over ice; squeeze in juice from lime wedges. Cover and shake. Strain into 2 martini glasses. Garnish with orange and/or star fruit slices (optional).

Petite Pear Puffs

Prep 20 minutes **Chill** 15 minutes
Bake 20 minutes **Cool** 5 minutes
Makes 16 puffs

1   egg
1   teaspoon water
1   sheet puff pastry, thawed, *Pepperidge Farm*®
5   tablespoons plus 1 teaspoon semisoft cheese with garlic
        and fine herbs, *Boursin*®
⅔   cup diced pears, drained and thinly sliced,* *Del Monte*®

1. Preheat oven to 400 degrees F. Line 2 baking sheets with parchment paper and set aside. For egg wash, in a small bowl, lightly whisk together egg and 1 teaspoon water. Set aside.

2. Unroll puff pastry sheet on a lightly floured surface. Using a rolling pin, roll puff pastry to a 14×10-inch rectangle. Using a sharp knife, cut into sixteen 3½×2½-inch rectangles.

3. Spread 1 teaspoon of the semisoft cheese in middle of a pastry rectangle. Top with 2 teaspoons of the pears. Using a pastry brush, brush egg wash around perimeter of the puff pastry rectangle. Bring corners of the pastry to the center and pinch seams together. Repeat to make 16 puffs. Arrange puffs, seam sides up, on prepared baking sheets. Refrigerate for 15 minutes. Remove from refrigerator and brush tops with remaining egg wash.

4. Bake for 20 to 25 minutes or until puffed and golden brown. Remove from oven and cool for 5 minutes. Serve warm.

*NOTE: Reserve remaining pears for another use.

Luscious Chocolate Martini

Start to Finish 5 minutes
Makes 2 servings

     Ice
2   shots Irish cream, *Bailey's*®
3   shots chocolate liqueur, *Godiva*®
2   shot hazelnut liqueur, *Frangelico*®
1   shot half-and-half or light cream
1   chocolate-covered candy bar stick, chopped,
        Butterfinger® *Stixx* (optional)

1. Fill a cocktail shaker with ice. Pour Irish cream, chocolate liqueur, hazelnut liqueur, and half-and-half over ice. Shake vigorously; strain into 2 martini glasses. Garnish with chopped candy bar stick (optional).

Sweet Pepper Poppers

Prep 25 minutes   Bake 20 minutes
Makes about 50 poppers

Olive oil cooking spray, *Pam*®
2   pints baby red, yellow, and orange bell peppers and/or
        jalapeño peppers (see note, page 77)
1   package (8-ounce) cream cheese, softened, *Philadelphia*®
2   scallions (green onions), finely chopped
1   cup shredded pepper Jack cheese (4 ounces), *Tillamook*®
1   cup fresh chunky salsa

1. Preheat oven to 300 degrees F. Lightly spray a baking sheet with cooking spray; set aside.

2. Cut each pepper lengthwise through stem. Using a spoon, scrape out seeds and veins. Set aside.

3. In a medium bowl, stir together cream cheese, scallion, and shredded cheese. Fill hollowed-out peppers with cheese mixture. Place peppers on a baking sheet. Bake for 20 to 25 minutes or until heated through. Top each pepper with a spoonful of the fresh salsa.

Cactus Rose Cocktail

Start to Finish 5 minutes
Makes 2 servings

Ice
½   cup frozen raspberries, *Dole*®
¼   cup frozen limeade concentrate, *Minute Maid*®
4   shots silver tequila, *Jose Cuervo*®
2   shots *Grand Marnier*®
2   shots cranberry juice cocktail, *Ocean Spray*®

1. Fill a blender with ice. Add raspberries, limeade concentrate, tequila, Grand Marnier®, and cranberry juice cocktail; blend until slushy. Pour into 2 margarita glasses.

Elegant Shrimp Rings

Prep 20 minutes **Freeze** 4 hours
Makes 15 servings

Pink grapefruit juice, *Ocean Spray*®

FOR PINK GRAPEFRUIT COCKTAIL SAUCE:
⅔ cup finely chopped refrigerated pink grapefruit segments, ***Del Monte*®**
½ cup chili sauce, ***Heinz*®**
2 tablespoons prepared horseradish, ***Morehouse*®**
¼ teaspoon celery salt, ***McCormick*®**

2 bunches fresh watercress
2 pounds large cooked shrimp with tails, thawed if necessary

1. Pour enough grapefruit juice into six 4-inch mini fluted tube cake pans to almost fill pans. Freeze for at least 4 hours, preferably overnight.

2. For Pink Grapefruit Cocktail Sauce, in a small bowl, stir together grapefruit segments, chili sauce, horseradish, and celery salt. Cover and refrigerate until ready to serve.

3. To serve, arrange watercress decoratively on a cake pedestal. Dip mini fluted tube pans in warm water just long enough for the juice rings to release from the pans. Place juice rings on watercress on pedestal. Place a long-stem cocktail glass onto center of pedestal. Fill bowl with Pink Grapefruit Cocktail Sauce. Arrange shrimp around ring.

Cherries Jubilee Cocktail

Start to Finish 5 minutes
Makes 2 servings

Ice
4 **shots vanilla vodka, *Smirnoff*®**
2 **shots cherry brandy, *Kirschwasser*®**
Lemon-lime soda, *Sprite*®
Maraschino cherries, *Mezzetta*®
Lemon and/or lime slices (optional)

1. Fill two cocktail glasses with ice. Pour 2 shots vodka and 1 shot cherry brandy over ice in each glass; stir. Top with lemon-lime soda. Garnish with cherries. Add lemon and/or lime slices (optional).

Crab Rangoon Cups

Prep 35 minutes   **Bake** 12 minutes
Makes 24 cups

¼   cup canola oil, *Wesson®*
24   wonton wrappers, *Dynasty®*
1   package (8-ounce) cream cheese, softened, *Philadelphia®*
1   can (6-ounce) lump crabmeat, drained, *Crown Prince®*
¼   cup canned white sauce, *Aunt Penny's®*
2   tablespoons chopped scallion (green onion)
1   tablespoon lemon juice, *Minute Maid®*
1   tablespoon Worcestershire sauce, *Lea & Perrins®*
½   teaspoon crushed garlic, *Gourmet Garden®*
¼   teaspoon dry mustard powder, *Coleman's®*
     Sliced scallion (green onion) (optional)

1. Preheat oven to 350 degrees F. Using a pastry brush, brush a thin layer of the oil in bottom and up side of each of 24 mini muffin cups. Set aside.

2. Brush wonton wrappers with oil and press into cups. Bake in preheated oven for 8 minutes or until lightly brown. Remove from oven and let cool in pans on wire rack.

3. In a medium bowl, combine cream cheese, crabmeat, white sauce, the 2 tablespoons scallion, lemon juice, Worcestershire sauce, garlic, and dry mustard, stirring until well mixed. Scoop 1 heaping tablespoon of crab mixture into each wonton cup.

4. Bake for 5 to 7 minutes or until filling is hot and edges are golden brown. Garnish with sliced scallion (optional). Serve warm.

Maui Sipper

Start to Finish 5 minutes
Makes 2 servings

     Ice
2   shots *Midori®* liqueur
1   shot coconut rum, *Malibu®*
1   shot *Cointreau®*
     Pineapple juice, *Dole®*
     Fresh pineapple wedges (optional)
     Pineapple leaves (optional)
     Orange slices, quartered (optional)

1. Fill two tall glasses with ice. Pour 1 shot Midori® over ice in each glass. Add ½ shot coconut rum and ½ shot Cointreau® to each glass. Fill glasses with pineapple juice. Garnish with pineapple wedges, pineapple leaves, and orange slices (optional).

Crispy Tortillas and Dip

Prep 25 minutes   **Bake** 8 minutes
Makes 1 ¾ cups

FOR CRISPY TORTILLAS:
4   garden spinach wraps, *Mission®*
4   sun-dried tomato basil wraps, *Mission®*
   Olive oil cooking spray, *Mazola® Pure*
   Kosher salt and black pepper

FOR DIP:
1   can (10.75-ounce) condensed creamy chicken soup, *Campbell's®*
1   package (8-ounce) shredded jalapeño Jack cheese, *Tillamook®*
½   cup sour cream
2   tablespoons green taco sauce, *La Victoria®*
1   tablespoon diced green chiles, *Ortega®*

1. For Crispy Tortillas, lay wraps on flat surface. Using a sharp knife, cut wraps into 2-inch-wide strips. Cut strips diagonally to form diamond shapes. Lay pieces in a single layer on a baking sheet. Lightly spray with cooking spray; sprinkle with kosher salt and pepper. Turn pieces over and repeat. Bake in preheated oven for 8 to 10 minutes or until pieces are crisp.

2. For Dip, in a medium saucepan, combine soup, cheese, sour cream, taco sauce, and chiles. Cook and stir over medium heat until smooth and heated through. To serve, arrange Crispy Tortillas on platter. Ladle the dip into a bowl and serve warm.

Cranberry Party Punch

Start to Finish 10 minutes
Makes 16 servings

4   cups cranberry juice cocktail, *Ocean Spray®*
2   cups black vodka, *Blavod®*
2   cups cherry brandy, *Kirschwasser®*
4   cups cola, *Coca-Cola®*
   Ice
   Maraschino cherries (optional)

1. In a punch bowl, combine cranberry juice cocktail, vodka, and cherry brandy. Slowly add cola. Serve over ice. Garnish with maraschino cherries.

Brilliant Bakery Embellishments

1. Create a star-studded dessert. Press chocolate stars, berries, or candies into the tops of frosted cupcakes to give them instant panache. Try the same trick on cakes and tarts.

2. Make purchased cookies special. Ice cookies with flavored, tinted frosting. Pipe initials or personal messages on top of the cookies with a pastry bag. Garnish with sprinkles and other candies.

3. Serve a sauce. Drizzle a chocolate or fruit sauce under servings of cheesecake, pie, and pastry. Dust the top of each serving with cocoa powder for an elegant presentation.

4. Make desserts fancy. Grate a softened chocolate bar with a vegetable peeler to make curls. Combine white and milk chocolate curls for a striking look.

5. Add flavor. Stir extracts, cinnamon, coffee powder, citrus zest, liqueurs, or cocoa into whipped topping for extra flavor.

The Recipes

Angel Food Tiramisu Cake

Start to Finish 25 minutes
Makes 10 servings

Tiramisu means "pick-me-up" in Italian, and that's exactly what mascarpone cheese, espresso powder, and Marsala wine do to a store-bought angel food cake. Dusting cocoa on top looks rich and adds a dash of extra flavor.

2	containers (3.75 ounces each) vanilla pudding snack cups, *Jell-O*®
2	containers (8 ounces each) mascarpone cheese,* softened
¼	cup Marsala wine, *Paul Masson*®
1	container (8-ounce) whipped topping, *Cool Whip*®
1½	cups warm water
¼	cup sugar
2	tablespoons instant espresso powder, *Medaglia D'Oro*®
1	store-bought angel food cake
	Cocoa powder (optional), *Hershey's*®

1. In a large bowl, combine pudding, mascarpone, and 2 tablespoons of the Marsala. Fold in whipped topping. Chill in refrigerator until ready to use.

2. On a rimmed baking sheet, combine the warm water, sugar, espresso powder, and the remaining 2 tablespoons Marsala.

3. To assemble, cut angel food cake horizontally into fourths. Dip both sides of bottom cake layer into espresso mixture and place on serving plate. Top with one-quarter of the mascarpone mixture. Repeat with the remaining cake layers and the remaining mascarpone mixture. Using a pastry brush, brush any remaining espresso mixture on sides of cake. Garnish with a dusting of cocoa powder (optional). Chill in refrigerator until ready to serve.

*****NOTE:** You can substitute cream cheese for the mascarpone cheese. The cake can be assembled up to 2 hours in advance.

Ambrosia Cake

Prep 20 minutes   **Bake** 6 minutes
Makes 12 servings

1	cup shredded coconut
1	12-ounce store-bought angel food cake
½	cup marshmallow creme, *Kraft®*
1	container (16-ounce) whipped topping, *Cool Whip® Extra Creamy*
1	can (8.25-ounce) peach slices, drained and cut in half, *S&W®*
1	can (8.25-ounce) sliced pears, drained and cut in half, *Del Monte®*
½	cup apricot preserves, *Smucker's®*
1	can (11-ounce) mandarin orange segments, drained, *Dole®*
1	can (8-ounce) pineapple slices, drained and cut in quarters, *Dole®*
¼	cup maraschino cherries, *Mezzetta®*

1. Preheat oven to 350 degrees F. Spread ½ cup of the coconut on a baking sheet in an even layer. Toast in preheated oven about 6 minutes or until golden brown. Remove from oven and set aside.

2. Cut cake into thirds horizontally. Place bottom layer on serving plate. Stir marshmallow creme into ½ cup of the whipped topping. Spread topping mixture on bottom layer; top with peaches and pears. Place middle layer on top. Spread preserves on middle layer and top with orange segments. Place top layer on top.

3. Frost entire cake with the remaining whipped topping. Toss the remaining ½ cup coconut with the toasted coconut; press into sides of cake. Arrange pineapple and cherries on top of cake. Refrigerate until ready to serve. Serve at room temperature.

Party Petits Fours

Start to Finish 30 minutes
Makes 16 petits fours

FOR CHOCOLATE-CHERRY FILLING:
¼   cup cherry preserves, *Smucker's*®
2   teaspoons crème de cacao, *Dubois*®

FOR PETITS FOURS:
8   slices store-bought chocolate marble loaf cake
8   slices store-bought lemon loaf cake

FOR GANACHE:
2   cups semisweet chocolate chips
1   cup whipping cream

FOR DECORATIONS:
1   can (16-ounce) chocolate or vanilla frosting, *Betty Crocker*®
     Chocolate-covered coffee beans
     Nut topping, *Planters*®

1. For Chocolate-Cherry Filling,* in a small bowl, stir together preserves and liqueur. Set aside.

2. Stack together 2 slices of the marble loaf cake. Cut the stacked slices into 1½-inch squares. Repeat with remaining marble loaf cake slices. Repeat procedure to make squares with the slices of lemon loaf cake. Spread a scant 1 teaspoon of the filling between layers of each square. Set aside.

3. In a medium microwave-safe bowl, combine chocolate chips and whipping cream. Microwave on high setting (100 percent power) for 1 to 2 minutes or until melted, stirring every 30 seconds. Place cake stacks on a wire cooling rack over waxed paper. Spoon Ganache over each cake stack until completely coated; allow excess Ganache to drip off. Transfer to a waxed paper-lined baking sheet. Chill until set. Fill a pastry bag fitted with a star or round tip (or use a heavy-duty zip-top bag with a corner snipped out) with chocolate or vanilla frosting; decorate cakes. Garnish with coffee beans and/or nut topping.

*BERRY FILLING: Omit Chocolate Cherry Filling. In a small bowl, combine ¼ cup seedless raspberry jam and 2 teaspoons crème de cassis. Continue as directed.

*ORANGE-APRICOT FILLING: Omit Chocolate Cherry Filling. In a small bowl, combine ¼ cup orange marmalade and 2 teaspoons apricot brandy. Continue as directed.

Banana Semifreddo

Prep 20 minutes   **Freeze** 4½ hours
Makes 8 servings

1½   cups whole milk
1   box (0.9-ounce) instant sugar-free banana pudding
          and pie filling, *Jell-O*®
2   small bananas, sliced ½ inch thick
2   cups store-bought chocolate or regular pound cake
1   pint black walnut ice cream, softened, *Häagen-Dazs*®
         Quartered strawberries (optional)
         Powdered sugar (optional)

1. Line bottom and sides of an 8½×4½-inch loaf pan with plastic wrap, leaving enough plastic wrap to hang over sides; set aside. In a large bowl, combine milk and pudding mix; whisk for 2 minutes. Let stand about 3 minutes or until thick.

2. Meanwhile, arrange banana slices on the bottom of the loaf pan, overlapping to make 2 layers if necessary. Spread banana pudding over bananas. Cover with plastic wrap and freeze for 30 minutes. Crumble pound cake over banana pudding and press down lightly. Spread ice cream over pound cake layer and smooth even with pan rim. Cover with plastic wrap and freeze about 4 hours or until firm. To remove, lift plastic wrap from pan. Invert onto serving plate. Garnish with strawberries and dust with powdered sugar (optional). Slice and serve immediately.

Mosaic Cake

Start to Finish 25 minutes
Makes 10 servings

This is one of my favorite desserts to make with my nieces and nephews. It couldn't be easier—just arrange packaged candies into a colorful design on top of a purchased cake. It adds a personal touch to birthdays or other occasions when you want to send a special message.

1	8-inch store-bought 2-layer cake (desired flavor), unfrosted if possible (or frosted white with simple design)
2	containers (12-ounce) vanilla whipped frosting, *Betty Crocker*®
1	bag (16-ounce) rainbow-colored candies, *Skittles*®

1. Scrape any design from top and sides of cake. Use 1½ containers of frosting to smoothly frost cake. Using a pastry bag fitted with a medium star tip, pipe the remaining half of a container of frosting onto the cake to make a shell border (optional). Store cake in refrigerator until ready to decorate.

2. Separate rainbow-colored candies by color. Select desired colors to use on your cake.

3. Find a picture template you like in a coloring book or magazine; cut out template. Place template cutout on top of frosted cake. Using a toothpick, trace outline of picture. Carefully remove template. Outline the major parts of the design with desired color of candy.

4. Fill in outline with candies to create picture, laying candies flat or on their sides to fit within the outlines. Create a border or background pattern with remaining candies in desired color (optional).

Anniversary Cheesecake

Start to Finish 20 minutes
Makes 22 servings

1	10-inch store-bought cheesecake, thoroughly chilled
1	8-inch store-bought cheesecake, thoroughly chilled
1	6-inch store-bought cheesecake, thoroughly chilled
1	can (12-ounce) chocolate frosting, melted, *Betty Crocker*®
	Assortment of fresh fruit (such as raspberries, blueberries, small clusters of red seedless grapes, blackberries, cranberries, and/or dark sweet cherries)
	Fresh mint sprigs (optional)

1. Place the 10-inch cheesecake on a cake plate or pedestal. Top with the 8-inch cheesecake. Place the 6-inch cheesecake on top of the 8-inch cake.

2. Carefully spoon melted chocolate frosting over each layer of the cheesecake. Arrange fruit on each cheesecake layer. Garnish with mint sprigs (optional). Chill until ready to serve.

TIP: To make the tiered cheesecake more stable, you can use three round cardboard cake cards (a 10-inch, 8-inch, and 6-inch) and six 3- or 4-inch-long plastic wedding cake columns (three for each layer) to assemble. Find wedding cake columns in the cake decorating department of hobby stores.

Individual Lemon Cheesecake and Blackberry Trifles

Start to Finish 25 minutes
Makes 4 servings

1	bag (16-ounce) frozen blackberries, thawed
6	tablespoons blackberry syrup, *Smucker's*®
2	cups milk
1	box (3.3-ounce) instant cheesecake pudding and pie filling, *Jell-O*®
½	cup lemon curd, *Dickinson's*®
2	cups store-bought pound cake cut into ¾-inch cubes, *Entenmann's*®
	Fresh blackberries and/or fresh mint sprigs (optional)

1. In a medium bowl, combine the blackberries and the blackberry syrup; set aside. In a large bowl, combine milk and pudding mix; whisk for 2 minutes. Let stand about 3 minutes or until thick. Spoon lemon curd into a small microwave-safe bowl; microwave on high setting (100 percent power) about 20 seconds or until pourable. Stir lemon curd into pudding until smooth.

2. Spoon ½ cup of the blackberry mixture into the bottom of each of four 8-ounce trifle dishes. Top each with ¼ cup of the pound cake cubes. Spoon lemon-cheesecake pudding on top of pound cake. Top with another ¼ cup pound cake cubes. Garnish with blackberries and mint (optional). Serve at room temperature or chilled.

Fast Fondant Cupcakes

Start to Finish 20 minutes
Makes 12 cupcakes

	Powdered sugar
1	box (24-ounce) ready-to-use rolled fondant (color multipack), *Wilton*®
12	store-bought bakery cupcakes, unfrosted*
¾	cup lemon frosting, *Betty Crocker*®

1. Sprinkle a little powdered sugar on a flat work surface. Using a rolling pin, roll out desired color of fondant to ¼-inch thickness, working quickly to prevent fondant from drying out (keep remaining fondant sealed in large zip-top bag until needed). Cut fondant into desired shapes with small cookie cutters or fondant cutters.

2. Frost each cupcake with 1 tablespoon of the frosting. Top with fondant cutouts.

*****NOTE:** If the cupcakes have frosting, carefully scrape it off each cupcake.

Cinnamon Roll Coffee Bombe

Prep 20 minutes **Freeze** 8 hours 45 minutes
Makes 10 servings

	Butter-flavor cooking spray, *Mazola® Pure*
20	(1 ounce each) pecan spinwheels, *Little Debbie®*
1	pint vanilla ice cream, softened,* *Dreyer's®*
1	cup chopped pecans, *Diamond®*
¾	cup butterscotch caramel sauce, *Mrs. Richardson's®*
1	carton (1.75-quart) coffee ice cream, softened, *Dreyer's®*
	Purchased caramel sauce (optional)

1. Spray a 2½-quart glass bowl with cooking spray. Cut spinwheels in half horizontally. Line bottom and sides of bowl with spinwheel tops (cut sides facing the inside of the bowl), pressing pieces closely together. Press spinwheel bottoms into holes between spinwheel tops to create a thick, solid outer layer.

2. Spread vanilla ice cream one-third of the way up the spinwheel-lined bowl, working quickly. Place in freezer for 30 minutes.

3. In a small bowl, stir together pecans and caramel sauce; spread pecan mixture in an even layer over vanilla ice cream. Freeze for 15 minutes.

4. Spoon coffee ice cream over caramel layer, smoothing ice cream even with bowl rim. Cover with plastic wrap and freeze about 8 hours or overnight.

5. Invert frozen bowl onto serving dish. Defrost on counter until bowl can be removed from bombe with ease. Drizzle with caramel sauce (optional). To slice bombe, dip a knife in hot water and cut into 10 slices, wiping knife clean after each cut. Serve immediately.

*****NOTE:** When working with the ice cream, it should be soft but not melted.

Sock-It-To-Me Individual Bread Puddings

Prep 20 minutes   **Soak** 15 minutes
Bake 35 minutes   **Makes** 6 servings

	Butter-flavor cooking spray, *Pam*®
1	**pound store-bought pound cake, cut into 1-inch cubes**
1	**cup chopped pecans, *Diamond*®**
¼	**cup packed brown sugar, *C&H*®**
2	**tablespoons ground cinnamon, *McCormick*®**
1	**cup milk or half-and-half**
¾	**cup egg substitute, *Egg Beaters*®**
¾	**cup sour cream**
1½	**teaspoons imitation butter flavor, *McCormick*®**
6	**tablespoons butter, cut into chunks**
	Powdered Sugar Glaze (optional)

1. Preheat oven to 350 degrees F. Spray six 4-inch ramekins with cooking spray and set aside.

2. In a large bowl, toss together pound cake cubes, pecans, brown sugar, and cinnamon until combined. Divide mixture among prepared ramekins.

3. In a medium bowl, whisk together 1 cup milk, the egg substitute, sour cream, and butter flavoring until well mixed. Pour ⅓ cup of the sour cream mixture into each ramekin. Soak for 15 to 20 minutes, occasionally pressing pound cake mixture into sour cream mixture.

4. Dot the top of each ramekin with 1 tablespoon of the butter chunks. Bake in preheated oven for 35 to 40 minutes.

5. Remove and cool slightly. Drizzle Powdered Sugar Glaze over puddings (optional). Serve warm.

POWDERED SUGAR GLAZE: In a small bowl, stir together 1 cup powdered sugar and 3 tablespoons milk until smooth.

Pineapples Foster over Warmed Doughnuts

Start to Finish 15 minutes
Makes 4 servings

I thought Bananas Foster was as good as it got until I tasted Pineapples Foster. Warm doughnuts melt in your mouth, leaving a spicy cinnamon afterglow. I like individual servings—they're more intimate and make people feel special.

6	tablespoons butter
6	tablespoons brown sugar, *C&H®*
8	canned pineapple slices, drained and chopped, *Dole®*
½	cup dark rum, *Myers's®*
2	teaspoons lemon juice, *Minute Maid®*
½	teaspoon pumpkin pie spice, *McCormick®*
4	store-bought glazed doughnuts
1	pint coconut sorbet, *Häagen Dazs®*

1. Preheat broiler. In a medium skillet, melt butter and brown sugar over medium heat. Simmer for 1 minute, swirling skillet frequently. Add pineapple; cook for 1 minute.

2. Remove from heat. Add rum, lemon juice, and pumpkin pie spice. Return skillet to high heat; boil about 1 minute or until sauce thickens. Remove from heat.

3. Place doughnuts on a baking sheet, spacing them 2 inches apart. Broil in preheated broiler 6 to 8 inches from heat for 2 minutes.

4. To serve, place 1 doughnut on each of 4 serving plates; top each with a scoop of the coconut sorbet. Spoon one-quarter of the pineapple mixture and sauce over top. Serve immediately.

Fondue Bar

Start to Finish 25 minutes
Makes 12 servings

FOR WHITE CHOCOLATE-BERRY FONDUE:

¾   cup heavy cream
3   bars (4 ounces each) white chocolate baking bar, cut into small
        pieces, *Ghirardelli*®
¼   cup amaretto, *Disaronno*®
⅔   cup blackberry spreadable fruit, *Smucker's*® *Simply Fruit*

FOR CHOCOLATE-CARAMEL FONDUE:

¾   cup heavy cream
3   tablespoons cognac
1   bag (12-ounce) semisweet chocolate chips, *Nestlé*®
½   cup butterscotch caramel sauce, *Mrs. Richardson's*®

FOR FONDUE BAR:

1   container (14-ounce) store-bought brownie bites
1   container (14-ounce) store-bought doughnut holes
    Assorted fresh fruit, such as strawberries and bananas
    Nut topping, *Planters*®
    Rainbow sprinkles, *Betty Crocker*®

1. For White Chocolate-Berry Fondue, in a small saucepan, heat cream over medium heat just until below a boil. Place white chocolate pieces in a medium bowl; pour hot cream over white chocolate pieces, stirring with a rubber spatula until completely smooth. Stir in amaretto and blackberry spreadable fruit until well mixed. Transfer to a 1½-quart slow cooker to keep warm or cover with plastic wrap and store until ready to serve.

2. For Chocolate-Caramel Fondue, in a small saucepan, heat cream and cognac over medium heat just until below a boil. Place chocolate chips in a medium bowl; pour hot cream-cognac mixture over chocolate chips, stirring with a rubber spatula until completely smooth. Stir in caramel sauce until well mixed. Transfer to a 1½-quart slow cooker to keep warm or cover with plastic wrap and store until ready to serve.

3. For Fondue Bar, on a serving plate, arrange brownie bites, doughnut holes, and fresh fruit; place toothpicks nearby. Pour nut topping and sprinkles into small individual serving bowls. Place warm Chocolate-Caramel Fondue and White Chocolate-Berry Fondue beside dippers and toppings. If desired, garnish White Chocolate-Berry Fondue with additional rainbow sprinkles. Spear desired dipper with toothpick; dip into desired fondue and sprinkle with desired topping.

Index

Index

Free
Lifestyle web magazine subscription

Just visit
www.semihomemade.com
today to subscribe!

Sign yourself and your friends and family up to the semi-homemaker's club today!

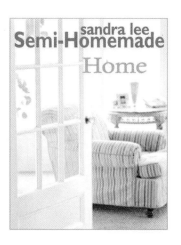

Each online issue is filled with fast, easy how-to projects, simple lifestyle solutions, and an abundance of helpful hints and terrific tips. It's the complete go-to magazine for busy people on-the-move.

tables & settings	fashion & beauty	ideas	home & garden	fabulous florals
super suppers	perfect parties	great gatherings		decadent desserts
gifts & giving	details	wines & music	fun favors	semi-homemaker's club

semihomemade.com
making life easier, better, and more enjoyable

Semihomemade.com has hundreds of ways to simplify your life—the easy Semi-Homemade way! You'll find fast ways to de-clutter, try your hand at clever crafts, create terrific tablescapes or decorate indoors and out to make your home and garden superb with style.

We're especially proud of our Semi-Homemakers club: a part of semihomemade.com which hosts other semihomemakers just like you. The club community shares ideas to make life easier, better, and more manageable with smart tips and hints allowing you time to do what you want! Sign-up and join today—it's free—and sign up your friends and family, too! It's easy the Semi-Homemade way! Visit the site today and start enjoying your busy life!

Sign yourself and your friends and family up to the semi-homemaker's club today!

| tablescapes | home | garden | organizing | crafts |

| everyday & special days | cooking | entertaining | cocktail time |

| Halloween | Thanksgiving | Christmas | Valentine's | Easter | New Year's |

Collect all of Sandra's books

Save Money ◆ Create More Time ◆ Make Life Easier

Also from Sandra Lee: *Made From Scratch, A Memoir*

More savvy solutions can be found online at *semihomemade.com*